HAVE WE

HAVE WE LOST OUR MIND?

THE CRAZY CONTRADICTIONS OF COSTLESS CHRISTIANITY

Larry E. Martin

RRMI
John 7:38

CHRISTIAN LIFE BOOKS
THE PUBLISHING ARM OF RIVER OF REVIVAL MINISTRIES, INC.
PENSACOLA, FL 32516

Copyright © 2013 by Larry Martin

ISBN 1-931393-32-X

CHRISTIAN LIFE BOOKS

P.O. BOX 36355
PENSACOLA, FLORIDA 32516
WWW.RRMI.ORG
WWW.AZUSASTREET.ORG
WWW.JESUS-IS-THE-ANSWER.COM

email: info@azusastreet.org

TABLE OF CONTENTS

I consider that the chief dangers that confront the coming century will be religion without the Holy Ghost, Christianity without Christ, forgiveness without repentance, salvation without regeneration, politics without God, and heaven without hell.

General William Booth

I am not afraid that the people called Methodists should ever cease to exist either in Europe or America. But I am afraid lest they should only exist as a dead sect, having the form of religion without the power. And this undoubtedly will be the case unless they hold fast both the doctrine, spirit, and discipline with which they first set out.

John Wesley

PREFACE

Roger Quesenberry is a friend of mine. He is the pastor of First Assembly of God in Walterboro, South Carolina.

When Roger was a boy, his father bought him a brand new left-handed baseball glove. Roger was so proud of that glove. He took the glove to baseball practice and a lad named Jimmy, one of his friends, stole it.

Roger went to where the boy lived in an apartment over a pool hall. He stood on the street below the apartment and shouted, "Jimmy, I want my glove back. I know you stole my glove and I want it back."

The boy wouldn't come down.

Undeterred, Roger kept yelling. Jimmy's mother came downstairs and told Roger to go home. No way, Roger wasn't going to budge. He wanted his glove back.

Bothered by all the commotion the men in the pool hall came out and told Roger to go home. He wouldn't hear it. No intimidation was going to hush him. Roger kept up his rant, "I want my glove back."

Finally, realizing that Roger was never going to give up, Jimmy opened a window and tossed the glove out on the street.

Roger went home . . . with his new glove!

We are living in a time when the devil has stolen a great deal from the church. I want it back.

Pentecostal churches in America once paid a high price for revival and saw God move powerfully, changing millions. Now it seems the movement has headed down a path of compromise and demise. We have already lost a lot. Often, it seems we have lost our mind.

Have we learned nothing from all the other revival movements that lost their way? Apparently not! In fact, it seems the Pentecostal movement is marching toward irrelevance at a faster pace than most of its predecessors.

I want it back.

This book is a call to repentance. It is a call to commitment. It is a book for everyone, but not everyone will like it. Some will hate it. Some will hate me. Too often when you uncover a problem, you become the problem.

Thousands have enjoyed my books on the Pentecostal past. Some will not be as enthusiastic about the Pentecostal present and future.

I will be called old fashioned. I will be called a legalist. I may be called worse. I will be criticized. I won't like it, but I am not going home. I want it back. The only way to get it back is repentance, commitment and self-denial.

I am a conservative, I am not a traditionalist. I do not want to go backwards. Andy, Aunt Bea, Opie, Barney, Goober, Gomer, Floyd, and even Ernest T. Bass were great. But, they are gone, as are the times in which they lived. Ward, June, Wally and the Beaver are never coming back. Neither is church-life as we knew it in the fifties and sixties. As precious as those memories are to me, I don't want to go back.

I want to go forward. I simply believe the way forward must not be paved with compromise. I want to see the church go forward with the same level of sacrifice and consecration that our fathers knew and experienced.

The English philosopher and author G.K. Chesterton wrote, "Compromise used to mean that half a loaf was better than no bread. Among modern statesmen [dare we insert *churchmen*?] it really seems to mean that half a loaf; is better than a whole loaf." Many of us know better. I am tired of half-loaf, watered-down, compromised Pentecostalism.

If you are tired of watching the greatest movement in the history of the Christian church turned into a religious circus; if you are tired of seeing essential doctrines and convictions compromised; if you have had enough of Pentecostal leaders who are leading in the wrong direction, come join me in the journey.

It might cost you something. No, without a doubt, it will cost you something. It will be worth it.

Let's take it back!

Larry Martin, D.Min.
Pensacola, Florida

Are the things you're living for worth Christ dying for?

Leonard Ravenhill

And David, according to the saying of God, went up as the LORD commanded. And Araunah looked, and saw the king and his servants coming on toward him: and Araunah went out, and bowed himself before the king on his face upon the ground. And Araunah said, Wherefore is my lord the king come to his servant? And David said, To buy the threshingfloor of thee, to build an altar unto the LORD, that the plague may be stayed from the people. And Araunah said unto David, Let my lord the king take and offer up what seemeth good unto him: behold, here be oxen for burnt sacrifice, and threshing instruments and other instruments of the oxen for wood. All these things did Araunah, as a king, give unto the king. And Araunah said unto the king, The LORD thy God accept thee. And the king said unto Araunah, Nay; but I will surely buy it of thee at a price: neither will I offer burnt offerings unto the LORD my God of that which doth cost me nothing. So David bought the threshingfloor and the oxen for fifty shekels of silver.

2 Samuel 24:19-24

WHAT DID IT COST YOU TO BE A CHRISTIAN THIS WEEK?

Ask the average church member, "What did it cost you to be a Christian this week?"

Chances are you will get answers like these . . .

Jesus died on the cross to cleanse me from my sins . . .

Jesus bore stripes on His back to pay for my physical healing . . .

Jesus went to heaven to baptize me in the Holy Ghost.

Yet, this is not a question about what He did for you. This is a question about what you did for Him! What did it cost *you* to be a Christian this week?

But, some would argue, the gospel is free. Don't kid yourself. Grace is freely given, but nothing cost more than your salvation. We all know the most beloved passage in the New Testament, "For God so loved the world, that he gave his only begotten Son, that whosoever believeth in him should not perish, but have everlasting life" (John 3:16). But, do we know what it really means? God gave His Son!

Divinity became humanity. Jesus "made himself of no reputation, and took upon him the form of a servant, and was made in the likeness of men: And being found in fashion as a man, he humbled himself, and became obedient unto death, even the death of the cross" (Philippians 2:7,8). Jesus Christ, God's Son died that you could have life. There could be no greater cost than that. But, once again, that is what He did for you. That is what it cost Him for you to be a Christian. What did it cost you, today?

Leonard Ravenhill, the great prophet with a pen, asks from the grave, "Are the things you're living for worth Christ dying for?"

In America, today, does it really cost anything to be a "Christian?" The Western church has done a pretty good job of blending with the popular culture. Church members and the unchurched go to the same theaters and listen to the same profanity. They watch the same television trash filled with sexual innuendo. With their remote controls church members vote for homosexual-promoting and family-damning Hollywood hell.

When most church members enjoy their musical collection, what songs do they choose? Are their choices any different from the unchurched? Of course not, how could we expect otherwise? Contemporary churches use the same unsanctified music in their "worship" services.

Simple Church, a growing mega-church in Shreveport, Louisiana started their Easter service with a dance video that sought to find the Elvis "mojo." Members of the church, dressed in everything from short shorts to bunny ears, danced, twisted and gyrated across the platform to a medley of godless music from "You Ain't Nothin' but a Hound Dog" to "Tonight's Gonna Be a Good, Good Night." Lyrics to some of the songs go beyond provocative to almost pornographic. All this is done to make the unchurched feel "comfortable."

In five years, there has never been an altar call in the church. One member told the *Shreveport Times,* "There's no pressure about anything. It's kind of on your own terms." Have we lost our mind?

Recently, while traveling, I passed a winery that advertised, "A taste of heaven without leaving the earth." Isn't this exactly what many churches are peddling today? Come to our church, get a little heaven without leaving the earth and its lusts.

In sharp contrast, Evangelist D. L. Moody wrote, "If I walk with the world, I can't walk with God." Who are you walking with?

The church no longer confronts popular culture, it doesn't even want to. It costs much less just to reflect culture. Does it really cost anything to be a Christian in our American religious culture?

In the last century famed pastor and author A. W. Tozer wrote, "Religion today is not transforming the people—it is being transformed by the people. It is not raising the moral level of society—it is descending to society's own level and congratulating itself that it has scored a victory because society is smilingly accepting its surrender." What would Tozer say today?

In Texas there is a church named "Thirty Minute Church." Their goal is get people into their church for thirty minutes a week. The whole program is abbreviated—a couple minutes for worship; a couple minutes for preaching. To ask today's Christians to give God more than thirty minutes is asking too much.

Not to be outdone—or is it undone—a church in Ireland has pared their weekly meeting to a measly twenty minutes. Can anyone get it down to five minutes? Or is five minutes to much to give God?

These example may be extreme, or are they? Fifty years ago Pentecostal churches met not only on Sunday morning, but as often as four nights every week for services that often lasted for hours. Now most have whittled that down to only one night with a promise of food and fun to draw a disinterested few.

Where have revival meetings gone? Just a short time ago most churches in America would host evangelistic meetings several times every year. These were not a two-day affair—they often went every night and lasted for several weeks at a time. Now many pastors lament, "I am afraid to schedule anything except Sunday morning, my people won't come." It costs too much to have revival today. Going to church two nights in a row (let alone seven) is too high a price to pay for culturally-relevant Christians. Does it really cost anything to be a Christian in America today?

Today's church members go from week to week without mentioning His holy name except on Sunday in church. In schools, in business, at work, His name seldom comes to mind and almost never crosses the lips. The unchurched use His name more often and more sincerely in their cursing and swearing than most Christians do in witnessing or testifying. Where is the societal stigma? What did it cost you to be a Christian this week?

Mormon youth give two years of their lives pedaling around the world on bicycles spinning Joseph Smith's yarns. As I travel the world, I see them—deceived youth deceiving others.

Jehovah Witnesses pound the pavement preaching their cultic propaganda. With their psuedo-bible and *The Watchtower* in hand, they regularly ring my doorbell in Pensacola. Where are the Pentecostals? Where are the Baptists? Where are the Methodists?

That kind of disciplined service is way too demanding for today's church. Western Christians had rather relax within their four walls, promoting happy, clappy gospel shows. Is it any wonder the church is in decline?

One of the most popular preachers in America appeared on nationwide television and was asked if Jesus was the only way to heaven. A boy or girl in a primary Sunday school class could answer that question, but Christianity's rising star couldn't even generate enough courage and conviction to say that atheists were not going to heaven. Making a stand for biblical truth might cost him something— royalties from books, television viewers, popularity, acceptability. In today's Christianity that would be too high a price to pay. Perhaps any price is too high. It does not cost much to be a Christian in America today.

It was not always this way.

The heart of true Christianity is in the prayer of the Seventeenth-Century Puritan pastor, Richard Baxter, "Lord, whatever you want, and whenever you want it, that's what I want." Baxter was a *real* Christian. Living for Christ cost him something. He was arrested often, fined frequently and imprisoned many times. Still, he wanted God's will more than his own.

Also a poet, Baxter penned:

Lord, it belongs not to my care,
Whether I die or live;
To love and serve Thee is my share,
And this thy grace must give.

If death shall braize this springing seed,
Before it come to fruit;
The will with Thee goes for the deed,
Thy life was in the root.

Thou lead'st me through no darker rooms
Than Christ went through before;
He that into thy kingdom comes,
Must enter by this Door.

Does it really cost any less to be a Christian in the twenty-first century?

When David prepared to make a sacrifice to end the plague of 2 Samuel 24 he needed a place to build an altar and offer a blood sacrifice to stay the hand of God's judgment. Araunah offered to give David anything he needed, completely free and without charge. David refused the generosity, declaring he would not present an offering to God that had cost him nothing. The situation was too grave, the need too great to give God a shoddy, contemptible offering. Lives were at stake. David knew that what cost him nothing was worth nothing.

Nearly five hundred years ago, the great reformer Martin Luther said, "A religion that gives nothing, costs nothing, and suffers nothing, is worth nothing."

How gladly do today's church members give a costless and worthless offering to God. They ignore the contradictions between true Christianity and their uncommitted lives. The fact is, many will only follow Him if it costs them very little or nothing at all.

Maybe—and only God will ultimately judge—but, *maybe* the Christianity they have is worth everything it costs them.

I beseech you therefore, brethren, by the mercies of God, that ye present your bodies a living sacrifice, holy, acceptable unto God, which is your reasonable service. And be not conformed to this world: but be ye transformed by the renewing of your mind, that ye may prove what is that good, and acceptable, and perfect, will of God.

Romans 12:1-2

IT WAS NOT ALWAYS THIS WAY

In the New Testament, Christianity cost something. According to church history and tradition all of the faithful disciples except John died as martyrs. Even John was imprisoned and exiled on barren Patmos. These men did not die with mercy. They died horrible deaths, suffering terribly. Some were beaten, others were crucified in the most agonizing postures. One was even skinned alive. It cost these men a great deal to be Christians. What does it cost us?

One get-rich-quick preacher said if Paul had known what we know today he would not have had to suffer. Blasphemy! Paul knew what the contemporary church has forgotten—he knew that it cost something to believe in Jesus Christ. He was assaulted often; imprisoned frequently; beaten unmercifully; stoned to the point of death; and finally gave his head to Caesar's sword. His journeys were perilous; his safety often, if not always, threatened. Without cowardice or prejudice he confronted the religious and political culture of his day. Who could doubt that Christianity cost him a great deal? Yet, in reply he said that all he suffered didn't compare with what Christ had prepared for him. Paul knew that Christianity cost something, but was worth all it cost. What does it cost you?

Throughout church history there has been a price to pay for being a Christian. First-century Rome set Christians ablaze as human torches for no other reason than their unshakable faith in Jesus Christ. In the coliseum they died at the hands of gladiators, battled with carnivorous beasts and became food for Caesar's lions. Why did they suffer? Why did they die? For making the same claims that Christians now make—but they meant it—and it cost them something. No, it cost them everything! What did it cost you to be a Christian this week?

In days gone by, men and women paid the ultimate price for believing the gospel. With his neck chained to a stake, John Huss said, "In the same truth of the Gospel which I have written, taught, and preached . . . I am ready to die today." And, die he did, perishing in the flames of religious bigotry. It cost Huss something!

John Wycliffe went to the stake for no greater crime than daring to challenge the religious establishment by translating the scriptures into a language common people could understand. A small crime by today's standards but a great sacrifice, especially now when Christianity costs so very little.

John Bunyan languished for years in Bedford prison simply because he refused to accept the government's standards for preaching the gospel. He could have compromised and been set free. He knew true Christianity cost something and he was ready to pay, whatever the cost.

There has never been a period of Christian history when wearing the name of Jesus Christ was as cheap as in today's western church. Does it cost anything?

Early Pentecostals paid a great price for embracing New Testament Christianity. They were criticized and ostracized. At Azusa Street, Henry McClain spent thirty days sleeping in a crowded jail and working on a chain gang. Why? For having a prayer meeting in his home that disturbed the neighbors. How many Pentecostals today would have a prayer meeting in their home, never mind disturbing the neighbors? That might cost something and most would be more concerned about their neighbors than their prayers.

What did it cost you to be a Christian this week?

F.F. Bosworth, an early Pentecostal and healing evangelist was once accused of mixing the races in a Texas meeting. His life was threatened and he was ran out of the town. Waiting at the train depot he was beaten nearly to death by an angry mob. Having missed the train, he was forced to walk to the next station. His Christianity had cost him something. Bosworth looked back on the night and said he was glad he had missed the train, it gave him opportunity to walk the rails in the moonlight and reflect on how blessed he was to suffer in Jesus name. Suffer? Not in today's church—that costs too much.

Even today, while the Western church peddles a pusillanimous gospel without cost, thousands of Christian around the world are suffering and dying for their faith. Believers across the globe are dying for Christ while many in America can't even pretend to live for Him.

Christians in desperate places and harsh conditions are starving for a lack of essential food while America's prosperity-promoting preachers live in multi-million dollar mansions and flit around the nation in their private jets. Can anyone see the indefensible contrast? Does it cost nothing to be a Christian in America today?

An American pastor told of hosting a guest minister from one of the former Soviet satellites. He was lamenting the fact that the forecast contained rain and the church people would not come to the meeting. He lightly remarked, I guess you have the same problem in your country. In a stinging reply the guest said in my country in intense cold and with two foot of snow a father will shovel a path for two miles so his family can follow him to church.

What did it cost you to be a Christian this week? What did you put on the line for the gospel of Jesus Christ? Is the life you are living worth Jesus dying for?

In 1776 American patriots pledged their lives, their liberty and their sacred honor to the cause of freedom. It was not a shallow pledge. It cost them something. Many lost lives; many lost family members; most lost their fortunes and their's were large fortunes at that.

Visit their graves some day. Every American should stand in a Revolutionary War Cemetery, it is sacred ground. The cost was enormous. Yet these brave men never flinched. They never looked back. What they believed was not only worth living for, it was worth dying for.

When Washington and his brave soldiers crossed the icy Delaware on Christmas Day 1776 they were facing impossible odds. Grossly outnumbered and under provisioned many of Washington's troops were ill, some had no warm clothes and more than a few didn't even have shoes for their frozen feet. As these gallant men, soaked by freezing rain, marched on the snow and ice in frigid temperatures, their path could be traced by the bleeding feet of shoeless colonists. Their chances for conquest were too minuscule to measure. Their chances for survival were slim, and many thought none. Still they marched on toward Pennsylvania. "Victory or death," was their slogan. They were willing to give their all.

What did it cost you to be a Christian this week? Is your faith in Him worth dying for? Is it worth living for?

A few churches talk about revival these days. We give thanks to God for all He is doing. But, why are so many pews empty? Great revivals are always accompanied by a great harvest. Where is the harvest today? Why is Christianity in America in decline? Why is it losing ground? Why are some calling this the era of Post-Christian America?

Could it be because Christianity cost little or nothing to most church members this week?

G. Campbell Morgan said, "The reason why men do not look to the Church today is that she has destroyed her own influence by compromise."

How many Christian's eyes were red from weeping over the lost today?

How many Christians fasted even one of their 21 meals this week?

How many turned off the television for even 30 minutes for personal devotions?

How many witnessed to even one person this week? This month? This year?

How many put their reputation on the line for the cause of Christ?

What did it cost you to be a Christian this week?

When it comes right down to it, there is only one thing God really wants from you. Heaven is not bankrupt—God can make it without your money. Believe it or not he doesn't need your charm and wit. Your education, as impressive as it may look on a resume, means nothing to Him. He doesn't care who baptized you, where you were dipped or which denomination you claim. He wants none of that.

God wants you—He wants all of you. That, you see, is what it costs you to be a Christian. In our day of shoddy salvations and bargain-basement baptisms and cheap conversions, the price of true Christianity is the same. To be a sincere follower of

Christ will cost you everything. That, friend, is what real Christianity will cost you this week.

Hymn writer, Elisha A. Hoffman spoke to an earlier generation with these penetrating words:

Is your all on the altar of sacrifice laid?
Your heart does the Spirit control?
You can only be blest,
And have peace and sweet rest,
As you yield Him your body and soul.

In Romans 12:1 Paul wrote, "I beseech ye therefore brethren by the mercies of God that you present your bodies a living sacrifice unto God, holy, acceptable, which is your reasonable service."

A sacrifice is not a curtsy or a tip of your hat to God. It is not a chintzy offering or even a tithe. A sacrifice is not a thirty minute service on Sunday morning. A sacrifice is death. God wants you dead!

Yet, God wants you alive. Sound contradictory? Such are the contradictions of true biblical Christianity. A believer in Jesus Christ is a living dead man. Alive in Him but dead to all else.

Dead to the world.

Dead to pride.

Dead to selfish ambitions.

Dead to respectability.

Dead to the popular culture, the religious culture and the political culture. That is what God expects from you. That is what it costs to be a Christian this week.

"Unreasonable," you say. Unreasonable in our present environment? Perhaps. Unreasonable in today's user-friendly and seeker sensitive churches? Probably.

Unreasonable to God? No, a thousand times no. God said that giving yourself to Him is your reasonable service.

Churches sing a little chorus that says, "When I think about His goodness and what He's done for me . . ." and then it goes through a litany of worshipful responses . . .

"It makes me want to shout."

"It makes me want to sing."

"It makes me want to dance."

Let's get real for a minute. Anybody can shout. Anybody can sing. Anybody can dance. You don't have to be a Christian to sing, shout and dance. It costs nothing!

The song of the church should be "When I think about His goodness and what He's done for me, I am going to present my body as a living sacrifice on the altar of God." Dead to self; alive in Him.

The nineteenth century Scottish minister, Robert Murray McCheyne wrote, "We do not know the value of Christ, if we will not cleave to Him unto death!" McCheyne died at twenty-nine years of age, totally burned out for Christ. His reward is in heaven.

Considering the price Jesus paid on the cross, every believer should live a dedicated life, committed totally to Him and His work. Every Christian should give Him *everything*. That is reasonable service! That is what it costs to be a true disciple of Christ.

It is unreasonable to give Him only a token. It is unreasonable to say I am a Christian but I still want to be popular. It is unreasonable to say I am a Christian but I don't want to force my faith on others. It is unreasonable to say I am a Christian but I don't want people to think I am a fanatic. It is unreasonable to say I am a Christian but I don't have time for Christ and His church.

That is giving God something that cost you nothing.

Pentecostal pioneer and Azusa Street participant, Frank Bartleman wrote, "All believers are called to a one hundred percent consecration . . . Our bodies are the temples of the Holy Ghost, and we are to be one hundred per cent for him at all times. We belong to Him. He has created us and bought us back, redeemed us after we had mortgaged His property, not ours, to the devil. In no sense are we our own."

Tozer said, "It is either all of Christ or none of Christ. I believe we need to preach a whole Christ to the whole world—a Christ who does not need our apologies, a Christ who is not divided, a Christ who will either be Lord of all or will not be Lord at all."

Is He Lord of all? Lord of *your all*?

What did it cost you to be a Christian this week?

Then said Jesus unto him, Put up again thy sword into his place: for all they that take the sword shall perish with the sword. Thinkest thou that I cannot now pray to my Father, and he shall presently give me more than twelve legions of angels? But how then shall the scriptures be fulfilled, that thus it must be?

Matthew 26:52-54

WHAT HELD JESUS TO THE CROSS?

What so many are willing to pay so very little for today, cost Christ so very much. What did it cost *Him* for you to be a Christian? Everything!

Someone manufactured and marketed a catchy little motto, "Nails didn't hold Jesus to the cross." Have you ever thought about that?

There were definitely nails. Archaeologists have found many examples of first century crucifixion nails. The most notable was from the tomb of a young man named Jehohanan. His skeletal foot still held the rusted Roman nail. The four and a half inch spike with a large head was driven from side to side through his heel. Evidence indicated a block of wood was placed between the head of the nail and the heel to better fasten the suffering victim to his cross.

Jesus had similar nails in his hands and his feet. But those nails didn't hold him to the cross.

The Romans were experts at crucifixion. Not all men were nailed to crosses, some were tied with ropes. Even many that were nailed were also tied. At times the nails may have been driven above the wrists in the carpal tunnel. If they were hammered into the palms of the hands, the flesh would not be strong enough to bare the weight of a grown man's limp body. Ropes would secure the arms if the nails didn't.

Ropes didn't hold Jesus to the cross.

The Roman Empire was as cruel as it was expansive. Through his emissaries and puppet kings Caesar held his conquered minions with a tight, iron fist. No one knows how many thousands were murdered by the Roman armies. A very conservative estimation puts the number of crucifixions at 10,000. It was probably thousands more. In one day 2,000 were crucified simply for the amusement of Quintilius Varus. When Israel fell to the Romans in 70 A.D., it is believed the foreign conquerors sent as many as five hundred Jews per day to the crosses outside Jerusalem. Caesar was a vicious tyrant and Rome was savage in her brutality, but neither Caesar nor Rome held Jesus on the cross.

Jesus said he could have called twelve legions of angels to free him from his suffering. The number of soldiers in a Roman legion varied with the times and with fluctuating circumstances, but it was roughly five thousand men. One assumes when Jesus referenced a "legion" of angels He had the same number in mind. Twelve legions of angels would be roughly 60,000. The destructive ability of a single angel is revealed in II Samuel 24:15 when one angel killed 70,000 men in three days.

Take a look at the math . . . it will amaze you. If one angel killed 70,000 people in seventy-two hours, he could kill 972 people in an hour. That is one man every three and a half seconds. This means twelve legions, or 60,000 angels could destroy more than sixteen thousand people every second--nearly 60 million in an hour. At this time, the population of the entire Roman Empire was estimated to be only about 45 million. Twelve legions of angels could have wiped the Roman Empire from the planet in less than one hour.

The late Ray Overholt penned it in verse so that millions could sing, "He could have called ten thousand angels to destroy the world and set him free. He could have called ten thousand angels but he died alone for you and me." No, the nails did not hold Jesus to His cross. Ropes did not hold Him. Romans did not Him hold to the cross.

So, what held Jesus to that cross?

He knew it pleased the Father. In John 8:29, Jesus said, "I do always those things that please him." Again, he said, "For I came down from heaven, not to do mine own will, but the will of him that sent me" (John 6:38). Jesus lived His life to please God. Nothing was more important to Him. He would be obedient, regardless of the cost.

Many Christians today think little of pleasing God. Many never concern themselves with obedience to His will. That might cost too much in our "It's-all-about-me culture." For many churchgoers the will of God falls low on the priority list—if it is a priority at all. Why pray about where to attend church? It is much simpler to find the church that has the most entertainment, the best trinkets for the kids and newest cappuccino machine. Is the will of God even a consideration?

Even clergymen are caught up in the selfish, humanistic religious race. One Pentecostal pastor quipped, "If it isn't good for me, it isn't good." Where can I please God is often secondary to the best salary and benefit packages. Often pastors refuse to leave an unproductive pastorate until they run the church completely into the ground, greedily hanging on for next week's check or holding out for retirement.

Baptist Pastor Chuck Baldwin lamented, "A good many religious leaders and churchmen today would not take a back seat to the most greedy, corrupt politician, or shady businessman that could be found." What a shame!

There *is* a perfect will of God for every life. Happy is the person who finds it and obeys it, regardless the cost.

Jesus obeyed the Father. "Lo, I come to do thy will, O God" (Hebrews 10:9).

In Gethsemane Jesus struggled. You would have struggled, too. Any man would have. The Master faced a bitter cup. Look what was before Him—the unspeakable pain of crucifixion; the humiliation of hanging naked on the cross; the rejection by His own people.

The cost was staggering.

Dietrich Bonhoeffer, a martyr in Nazi Germany, said, "You can only learn what obedience is by obeying."

Jesus obeyed. Despite the horrific cost, He said not my will. Obedience is not relevant until it is expensive. Anyone can call Him "Lord" when it costs nothing. But how about when He asks you to follow a path that will cost you something—or everything!

"Partial obedience is not obedience at all," wrote Seventeenth Century Puritan Richard Sibbes, "to single out easy things that do not oppose our lusts, which are not against our reputation, therein some will do more than they need; but our obedience must be universal to all God's commandments, and that because He commands it. Empty relationships are nothing; if we profess ourselves God's servants and do not honour Him by our obedience, we take but an empty title."

Tozer wrote, "Salvation apart from obedience is unknown in the sacred Scriptures. Apart from obedience there can be no salvation, for salvation without obedience is a self-contradictory impossibility."

Before his conversion, Fred Orr was a noted football player in his native Belfast. Surrendering to God also meant surrendering to a missionary call to the jungles of Brazil. It was a custom at the time that churchgoers would gather at the Irish port and bid farewell to outgoing missionaries. A good group joined Fred and his wife, Ina, as they left for the Amazon in 1954.

Orr asked the Pentecostal evangelist, Billy Waters to stand on the docks and sing, "I Have Decided to Follow Jesus." The rugged Irishman stood and sang his anthem as the Orrs sailed toward their new home.

The world behind me, the cross before me;
The world behind me, the cross before me;
The world behind me, the cross before me;
No turning back, no turning back

I have decided to follow Jesus;
I have decided to follow Jesus;
I have decided to follow Jesus;
No turning back, no turning back.

Orr had no idea how much obedience would cost him. After the long trek across the Atlantic the couple began a 2500 mile boat ride into the dense forests. Before they ever reached the mission station, Ina contracted a deadly fever. Without even one English speaking companion to give him comfort, Orr buried his young wife on a river bank in Brazil. Obedience to God is costly. It costs Fred Orr a lot.

Fifty-seven years later, Orr also died in Amazonas, thousands of miles from his ancestral home. Many times while lonely and discouraged, Orr said he would hear Water's voice ringing in his ears, "No turning back . . . No turning back."

Have you decided to follow Jesus?

What if obedience costs you? What if it costs you a lot? Will you turn back?

James and Susan Dodd were quite comfortable. He pastored a great church he had pioneered some years before. She had worked hard to complete her education and was enjoying teaching school. Nearing fifty years of age, it was time to think about retirement and being at home with the grandchildren. But, God had another idea. James and Susan, obedient to the Father, left their comfort zone to become missionaries. That was hard . . . but life was about to get harder. While in language school in Costa Rica they got the call every parent fears. There was an awful automobile accident, their oldest daughter and a precious niece were killed. Their youngest girl was barely hanging to life. These godly girls were in Bible school preparing for Christian service. Now, they were gone. Doing the will of God is expensive. It will cost you something. It might not cost you as much as it cost James and Susan, but it will cost you. It cost Jesus everything. To Him, pleasing the Father was worth it. What is it worth to you?

Founder of the Salvation Army, William Booth said, "The greatness of a man's power is the measure of his surrender." Booth surrendered all.

Jesus was also held to the cross by His commitment to His own destiny. Jesus knew why He came to the earth. He had a divine destiny. A higher will and purpose ordered His steps.

When Pilate asked Him if He was a king, Jesus answered, "Thou sayest that I am a king. To this end was I born, and for this cause came I into the world. . ." (John 18:37). As He faced the immediacy of His suffering and death, He said, "Now is my soul troubled; and what shall I say? Father, save me from this hour: but for this cause came I unto this hour" (John 12:27).

No one else could fulfill His destiny. No one else can fulfill yours. You are here for a reason, a divine purpose. Hanging from the wall of many Grandmothers' homes this maxim screams at us today, "Only one life will soon be past, only what's done for Christ will last."

Fulfilling His destiny cost Christ His life. It will also cost you, but what is life without divine purpose? If your life costs nothing, it is probably worth nothing. Is the life you're living worth Christ dying for?

Mordecai Ham was the son and grandson of preachers. There were ministers in his lineage for eight generations. Early in his life he felt the call to preach. It seemed his destiny was already written in heaven. But young Mordecai had a better idea. He would create his own destiny.

Ham saw that the minister's life was one of deprivation and sacrifice. He had watched his own family barely eke out an existence. He wanted none of it. Mordecai went to college. He studied law but was too young to take the bar exam so he went into business. He worked for a picture enlargement company in Chicago. Life was good. But, how about his God-given destiny?

When Ham's grandfather died it was a life-changing moment for him. He said nothing in life convinced him more of the reality of the Christian faith than seeing his grandfather die. He saw an old man fulfill his destiny. Nothing else mattered. Money didn't matter. Success didn't matter. Mordecai Ham would fulfill his destiny.

He immediately resigned his work and began preparing himself for the ministry. Ham preached great meetings across the Southern United States and saw more than 300,000 people accept Christ as their Savior. This alone would satisfy any man. He knew his destiny and he fulfilled it.

But, wait, the story is not complete. In 1934, Ham was invited to conduct a crusade in Charlotte, North Carolina. The crusade committee approached Frank Graham about holding the meeting on his dairy farm. Graham gladly consented. His young son, Billy, attended the services and after several nights of resisting the Holy Spirit, answered the altar call and accepted Jesus Christ as his Savior and Lord. The rest, they say, is history. But is it?

What if Mordecai Ham had not surrendered to the call? What if he had chosen the easy path? What if he pursued a life of financial success? More than three million people responded to the invitation to accept Christ in Billy Graham's crusades around the world. Heaven must rejoice that Ham fulfilled his destiny.

Find your own personal God-given destiny and fulfill it—regardless the cost. If it is to be a good church member; a good mother, a good father, a good son; or, a good daughter, find it and do it with all your might.

Much more could be written on what held Jesus to the cross, but it would be too great an omission not to include His love for humankind. How else can it be said? Love held Jesus to the cross.

Jesus had an unending compassion for hurting humanity. That is why He came. That is why He healed the diseased and broken hearted. That is why He suffered. That is why He died.

He loves us—all of us. He did not die upon the cross just to save good people. He would say, those that are well don't need a doctor (Mark 2:17). No, He came to save the best of us and the worst of us. "While we were yet sinners, Christ died for us" (Romans 5:8).

> Could we with ink the ocean fill,
> And were the skies of parchment made,
> Were every stalk on earth a quill,
> And every man a scribe by trade;
> To write the love of God above
> Would drain the ocean dry;
> Nor could the scroll contain the whole,
> Though stretched from sky to sky.
>
> Oh, love of God, how rich and pure!
> How measureless and strong!
> It shall forevermore endure—
> The saints' and angels' song.

The word "love" has been cheapened in our modern vernacular. It often means no more than craven, selfish lust. Jesus demonstrated real love—the greatest love. He died for us. Do we not demean the word when we say we love Him and give Him nothing?

Nails did not hold Jesus to the cross; the Romans did not hold Him there. He was held by His love for men and women and His obedience to the Father's good will.

"God gives His own self totally to us," wrote Watchman Nee, "that we might offer ourselves completely to Him."

He was not compelled. He could have been freed from His awful fate. The angels were at His beck and call. He chose the cross.

Neither, are we compelled. We can choose a life without a cross. Many have. But doesn't real Christianity demand more? If pleasing the Father was enough to hold Jesus to the cross, will it not also constrain us? If His love for others cost Him everything, will our love then cost us nothing?

If you are truly His disciple, is it not reasonable to believe that what held Him to His cross will also hold you to yours? Remember, it wasn't nails that held Him to that cross.

Let this mind be in you, which was also in Christ Jesus: Who, being in the form of God, thought it not robbery to be equal with God: But made himself of no reputation, and took upon him the form of a servant, and was made in the likeness of men: And being found in fashion as a man, he humbled himself, and became obedient unto death, even the death of the cross. Wherefore God also hath highly exalted him, and given him a name which is above every name: That at the name of Jesus every knee should bow, of things in heaven, and things in earth, and things under the earth; And that every tongue should confess that Jesus Christ is Lord, to the glory of God the Father.

Philippians 2:5-11

THE CHRISTIAN *KENOSIS*

Theologians speak of the *"Kenosis* of Christ." *Kenosis* is a Greek word, meaning "emptiness" and is used to describe the attitude and actions of Christ during the incarnation. Various translators render verse seven as "Jesus made himself nothing;" "he emptied himself;" "stripped himself of all privilege;" and "he gave up his divine privileges."

There is nothing more significant than Christ becoming flesh and dwelling among men. To leave the splendors of heaven and dawn the robes of humanity was a demotion of the highest order. Jesus understood that personal sacrifice for the good of others is the most noble calling. Nothing can take away from His great sacrifice. Yet, it seems Philippians 2 is speaking more about our *kenosis* than His. "Let this mind be in you." says the

Apostle Paul. What mind? The same that was in Christ.

Don't misunderstand. No one could give more than Christ. He left heaven. Jesus showed us how different He was from satan. Satan filled with pride wanted to usurp the Most High God. Jesus showed how different He was from unredeemed humanity. Adam and Eve wanted to be "as gods." Jesus emptied Himself to be as man.

As Jesus emptied Himself, believers should also empty themselves. Pride must die. Greed must die. Lust must die. Ambition must die. The flesh must die. It costs something to "have this mind in you."

The Christian *Kenosis* includes several important elements. The first of which is humility. Jesus humbled Himself; Christians must humble themselves.

God hates pride.

Pride made a devil of an angel. The true believers empty themselves of this selfishness.

Many today have became wealthy preaching the gospel. They brag about their mansions, their luxury cars, their private jets and opulent lifestyles. God is not impressed. Others have abandoned their riches and lived on meager means to reach the lost. God must be very impressed. Surely this is the "same mind" Paul had in mind. This is the Christian *Kenosis*.

Dwight L. Moody was raised by a widowed mother in the deepest poverty. As he left home and started his career, he determined to never be poor again. His aspiration was to have $100,000 in personal wealth, a huge sum of money in the mid-nineteenth century and easily equal to a million dollars today. When he reached Chicago, he was well on his way to that goal. Finding his niche in the shoe business, he was earning $5,000 a year in commissions above his salary. This was in a time when a prosperous blacksmith made only $250 a year. Moody was a very wealthy man and he was using his money for the sake of the gospel. Every evening, every weekend and every spare minute he was involved in ministry.

Yet, that was not enough, Moody felt God was calling him to full-time service. This man of God resigned his job and emptied himself. Moody told one of his associates, "I have decided to give to God all my time." "But how are you going to live?" asked his friend. Mr. Moody replied, "God will provide for me, if he wishes me to keep on, and I shall keep on until I am obliged to stop."

Moody moved into the YMCA until all his savings were gone and then he slept on a bench in the prayer chapel. During a time when his faith was tried he lived only on crackers and cheese. At the same time Moody collected considerable finances for his mission work but kept not one cent for himself. Over a long career, Moody established several schools and published many books. He traveled a million miles and personally preached to 100 million people. God provided. With all his fame and acclaim, Moody lived a very humble life. The man who traveled so far died in his own modest home in Northfield, Massachusetts in view of the simple cottage where he was born.

Moody could have been a wealthy man. He could have saved the $100,000 he coveted as a youth. He could have; but, he didn't. In today's church culture "emptiness" is a contradiction. It costs too much. In heaven it is "this mind in you."

Billy Sunday was a noted baseball player when he began attending the Garden Street Rescue Mission in Chicago. The popular outfielder was the first player to run the bases in fourteen seconds. He played for Chicago, Pittsburgh and Philadelphia. Sunday had been out carousing with other team members when he heard a street preacher from the mission. The songs reminded him of his mother and he soon accepted Christ as his Savior.

Like Moody, Sunday was raised in poverty by a widowed mother. He even spent some of his childhood in an orphanage when his mother could no longer care for him and his older brother. While still a teenager Sunday began to play for hometown baseball teams. More than anything else, his ability to steal bases won him a position in the major leagues.

Sunday was good, if not excellent. As a professional athlete he was earning four hundred dollars a month—a tremendous salary considering the average annual income in America was less than five hundred dollars.

Feeling the call to full-time ministry, in 1891 Billy Sunday emptied himself. He left the lucrative sports field to take a ministry job that paid him only eighty-three dollars a month, a fraction of what he earned as an athlete. At one point Sunday was offered $2,000 a month to come back to baseball. For Sunday there was no turning back, not even when Hollywood offered him a million dollars to be in the movies.

Sunday was the most successful evangelist that had ever lived. In one of his crusades in Detroit, two million came to hear him preach and 200,000 were converted. When Sunday preached in Wilkes-Barre, Pennsylvania one-fourth of the city was converted. So many people stopped drinking alcohol that over the next year two hundred taverns closed their doors. According to the newspaper two years after the crusade 83% of Sunday's converts were still serving the Lord. Results like these followed Sunday for decades wherever and whenever he preached across the United States. As many as 1,200,000 accepted Christ in his meetings.

Sunday understood the *kenosis* of the Christian. Even as a highly successful evangelist, Sunday could have became a millionaire. His crusade offerings amounted to much more than that. Instead, Sunday gave most of his money away. When he preached a great crusade in Chicago, the offerings amounted to $58,000. He gave it all to the Pacific Garden Mission where he was converted. The contributions from his New York crusade totaled $120,500 all of which Sunday donated to war charities. He never lived an opulent life-style, even though he could have. His home was modest and his life was humble. "This mind," that was in Christ, was in Billy Sunday and he changed his world.

Unlike Moody and Sunday, C. T. Studd was from a very wealthy English family. His father had gained a fortune in India and had returned home to enjoy his riches, racing horses and gambling. That is, until he met D. L. Moody. The senior Studd accepted Christ and gave up his carnal pursuits. He took his three sons to hear Moody, but they resisted the Spirit's conviction. It was a year later that all three sons accepted Christ on the same day.

C. T. had become very popular as a cricket player. He captained the team at Cambridge and was one of the best cricket players in the world. C.T. Studd was quite likely the best known athlete in England.

And then Moody came to Cambridge. Studd heard the evangelist, recommitted his life and felt a call to China. The "emptying" of C. T. Studd had begun. He and six other students, known forever as "The Cambridge Seven" left a life of privilege to serve God on foreign soil.

On his twenty-fifth birthday, Studd inherited $145,000—quite a fortune for the late nineteenth century. Immediately Studd sent out checks for Christian work. Twenty-five thousand went to Moody and built the Moody Bible Institute; twenty-five thousand was to be used for ministry among the poor in London; George Mueller received twenty-five thousand, as did the Salvation Army in India. Others received smaller amounts, but in one day C.T. Studd emptied himself of $125,000.

When he was ready to marry, he had $17,000 remaining. He asked his bride-to-be what they should do with the money and she answered, "Charlie, what did the Lord tell the rich young man to do? Sell all. Well then, we will start clear with the Lord at our wedding." The remaining money went to the Salvation Army and they started their life together with five dollars and faith in God.

C.T. Studd had emptied himself. Like his master, he knew personal sacrifice for the good of others is the most noble calling. He had "this mind" in him.

Studd, however, gave more than his money. He gave his all. Having served successfully in China and then returning to England to promote the missionary work, at age fifty Studd felt a call to preach to the unreached people of Africa. He spent the last twenty years of his life largely separated from his family and working in the most difficult circumstances and among the most depraved and destitute people on earth. He suffered from dysentery, chills, gallstones and malaria, but would still preach through his pain for up to eighteen hours a day. He gave everything. He humbled himself. He emptied himself.

On the day of his eternal promotion, Studd used what little strength he could muster to repeat, "Hallelujah! Hallelujah!" In darkest Africa he had "this same mind." Earlier in his career, Studd said, "If Jesus Christ is God and died for me, then no sacrifice can be too great for me to make for Him." How much did it cost you to be a Christian this week?

Today, believers want a gospel that only gives something. Churches that make big promises of health and wealth are often full.

Noted author A. W. Pink said, "The first step toward a daily following of Christ is the denying of self." How many pastors preached that to their congregations last week.

The way of the cross is a way of humility.

Jesus not only humbled Himself, He was also obedient. The mind-set of many in the world is "Don't tell me what to do!" Sad to say, the same obstinate attitude permeates much of the church world.

Christ Jesus submitted Himself to the will of the Father. He could do nothing else.

Again, it was important that Jesus show us the difference in Himself and satan. Satan was a rebel. Jesus was obedient to the Father's will. Look at the contrast between Christ and the first human couple. They disobeyed. Christ obeyed.

The *kenosis* of Christ shows believers how to be obedient. The cross is a picture of Christian compliance.

Tozer said, "The man with a cross no longer controls his destiny; he lost control when he picked up the cross . . . No matter what he may desire to do, there is but one thing he can do; that is, move on toward the place of crucifixion."

There is a great story in I Samuel 13. The Philistines had gathered against the children of Israel to do battle. Saul grew impatient awaiting the arrival of Samuel so he took upon himself the priestly duties and offered the sacrifice. This showed a flagrant disregard for God's prescribed manner of worship.

Almost immediately Samuel appeared and Saul tried to explain. He blamed his impatience on the Israelites and in one of the poorest excuses in human history, he said "I forced myself." In other words, he didn't want to disobey, he had to force himself to do it.

Samuel was not impressed with the kings excuses. He told Saul he had acted like a fool and that if he had been obedient his kingdom would have lasted forever. Because he was disobedient, the kingdom would be taken from him.

A short time later, Saul again showed his insolence. Israel's King was going to battle against the Amalekites. God's directions to Saul were very clear. He was to utterly destroy all the Amalekites and everything they owned. Saul had a better idea. He destroyed everything that was worthless but saved the best of the sheep and cattle. He also kept Agag the king of the Amalekites as a trophy of war.

God spoke to the Prophet Samuel and told him that he was sorry that Saul had been appointed king and that he had not obeyed his direct command. Samuel was broken-hearted but he dutifully faced the king.

As Samuel approached Saul, he bragged, "I have kept the commandment of the Lord." Samuel rebuked the lying king, saying, "If you have kept the Lord's commandments, why do I hear the bleating of the sheep and the lowing of the oxen?"

Knowing he was caught, Saul replied, "We kept the best of the animals to sacrifice them to the Lord."

Samuel's response is one of the most poignant in the Bible, "To obey is better than sacrifice." Samuel told Saul that rebellion is like witchcraft and stubbornness is as sin and idolatry. Because of his disobedience, God rejected Saul as Israel's king. Obedience is costly. Disobedience costs even more.

Jesus' obedience cost Him everything. Had he not obeyed it would have cost us everything. Our salvation was dependent on His obedience. Thank God, He obeyed. Will this "same mind" be in you?

The *kenosis* of the believer involves humility and obedience. It demands more. It demands death.

There is no denying that Christianity is about living. In John 10:10, Jesus said, "I am come that they might have life, and that they might have it more abundantly."

There is also no denying that Christianity is about dying. Satan was obsessed with his life. Adam and Eve were consumed with their lives. It was all about them.

Jesus was consumed with our lives. He was born to die that man might live. If a believer die; if they are crucified with Him, then He lives in them. The more they are willing to die the more they live.

It is the paradox of the gospel. To keep one's life, it must be given away. A seed cannot live until it falls into the ground and dies. Jesus said those who love their lives will lose them. Those who hate their lives now, in this world, will keep their lives eternally (John 12:24-25).

"All God's plans have the mark of the cross on them, and all His plans have death to self in them." said E. M. Bounds, "But men's plans ignore the offence of the cross or despise it. Men's plans have no profound, stern or self-immolating denial in them. Their gain is of the world." Could the contradiction be more evident? Costless Christianity exists only with those who have lost their mind.

In Matthew 16:24, Jesus said, "If any man will come after me, let him deny himself, and take up his cross, and follow me." Taking up a cross does not mean carrying a wooden plank. Even though this has proven to be an effective means for evangelism, it is not what Jesus had in mind. Taking up a cross does not mean wearing jewelry on a chain around the neck or taking a "faith based" tattoo. Taking up a cross means death. It means dying to our wishes, our plans, our ambitions, our fleshly desires. This is "the mind of Christ" that should be in every believer—and it costs something.

Everyone wants to be an overcomer. Books about being an overcomer are best sellers. Many quote Revelation 12:1, "And they overcame him by the blood of the Lamb, and by the word of their testimony . . ." This verse is a favorite of the overcoming crowd. Few, however, quote the second part of the verse, ". . . and they loved not their lives unto the death." The real key to victorious living is dying, or at the least a willingness to die.

The more we die, the more we live.

This brings us to the final element of the *kenosis* of the Christian. After Christ's humility, obedience and death came His exaltation. Because Christ humbled Himself; because He was obedient; because He died on the cross, God exalted Him to reclaim all the privileges of His deity.

Again, note the contrasts. The devil was proud; he was disobedient; he sought *his* life; and, subsequently, his eternal destiny is punishment and banishment from the presence of God.

Sinful man, beginning with Adam and Eve, is proud, disobedient and selfish. The end of man's rebellion is destruction.

On the other hand, for the believer who is walking in humility; walking in obedience; and, dying daily, the end is exaltation. This, too, is the *kenosis* of Christ.

It cost something to be a true follower of Jesus Christ. For many it has cost everything. However, these trials are but for a season. Emptiness ends in fullness. God has prepared something great for the believer who has "this mind in him."

Walter J. Chantry, author of *The Shadow of the Cross*, explains, "Not one man has ever sacrificed for his Lord without being richly repaid. If the cross is only contrasted with earthly pleasures lost, it may seem hard and threatening. But when the cross is weighed in the balances with the glorious treasures to be had through it, even the cross seems sweet."

Remember, *kenosis* cost Paul everything. But it was this same apostle who reminds believers that all the emptiness, all the humiliation, all the obedience, even death wasn't worth comparing to the exaltation (Romans 8:18). Real Christianity costs something. But, it is worth whatever it costs.

Let this mind be in *you*, which was also in Christ Jesus. Anything less is not New Testament Christianity.

A church without the *kenosis* of Christ is a church that has lost its mind.

Or, has it just lost *His* mind?

Whatsoever thy hand findeth to do, do it with thy might, for there is no work, nor device, nor knowledge, nor wisdom, in the grave, whither thou goest.

Ecclesiastes 9: 10

Whether therefore ye eat, or drink, or whatsoever ye do, do all to the glory of God.

1 Corinthians 10:31

ARE YOU DOING YOUR BEST?

In 1972 the Summer Olympics were held in Munich, Germany. The games are best remembered for the senseless murder of eleven Israeli athletes and coaches by Palestinian terrorists. Athlete, actress and spokeswoman Cathy Rigsby remembers for another reason. In 1970 Cathy won the hearts of the American people by being the first American woman to ever win a medal in the world gymnastics competition. In 1972 Cathy was once again a member of the United States team and Cathy's goal was to take the gold medal. Prior to the games she had injured herself attempting a precarious maneuver on the balance beam. Despite the injury she had high hopes for the gold and prayed that God would help her. She did not want to disappoint herself, her team or her country. She performed well, but unfortunately not well enough. When the scores were announced she fell short not only of the gold, but of any of the other prized medals.

Cathy's dreams were shattered. Embarrassed by the loss she went to the bleachers where her parents were watching and rooting for her. Fighting back the tears she turned to her mother and said, "I'm sorry. I did my best." Her mother consoled her by saying, "You know that, and I know that, and I'm sure God knows that too." Then Cathy's mother told her something that has stuck with her for the past forty years, "Doing your best is more important than being the best." Amen.

There are several definitions of the word "best" depending on the context in which the word is used. The most appropriate for this context is "the supreme effort one can make." There can be a huge difference between being the best and doing your best.

Are you doing your best for Christ and His kingdom? None can doubt that He gave His best for you. Are you giving your best to Him?

The writer of Ecclesiastes said whatever we do we should do with our might. In other words we should do our best. Paul told us that everything we do should be done for the glory of God. If all our endeavors are to glorify God, can we glorify Him by giving less than our best? We should pursue all things with all our might.

Famed Baptist Pastor Jack Hyles said, "If a task is worthy of our attention, it is worthy of our best." Hyles spent years giving God his best and he built the largest Sunday school in America.

We should give our supreme effort to all our pursuits, but certainly to our pursuit of God. Doesn't He deserve our best? Doesn't He deserve *your* best?

Twentieth century martyr Jim Elliot challenged the church, "Wherever you are, be all there. Live to the hilt every situation that you believe to be the will of God." Are you in the will of God? Are you living your life to the hilt? Elliot did.

Noted philanthropist John D. Rockefeller, Jr. said, "The secret of success is to do the common things uncommonly well." Rockefeller watched his father become the richest man in the world by doing his best. Can a true Christian offer God any less?

Are you doing your best as a Christian?

Acts 11:26 says, "And the disciples were first called Christians in Antioch." It does not say they called themselves Christians, although that is possible. It is more likely that the heathen gave them that title. Why? The word "Christian" is *christianos* in the Greek language. It means "follower of Christ." It comes from the Greek word *christos* which means "anointed one" with a Latin adjective added at the end.

This was a common form of construction in that day. In ancient literature the army of Pompey was called *pompeyano*. Christian, then, could be the "army of Christ." But the adjectival ending means much more than just a soldier. It denotes adhering to and even *belonging* to. *Christianos* means belonging to Christ. It means ownership. It means slavery. Often, New Testament writers referred to themselves as "servants" or more properly translated "slaves" of Jesus Christ.

But, the question was "Why did they call them Christians?" There is only one answer. They were followers of Christ. They gave Him their best. They followed Him so closely, they obeyed him so fully, they were *like* His slaves. No, they *were* His slaves.

What if your friends, family and acquaintances knew that the word "Christian" implied being totally sold out to Christ. Would they call you a Christian? Would they think that you give Him your best?

"There is no such thing as part-time loyalty to Christ," said Vance Havner. "A wife who is 85 percent faithful to her husband is not faithful at all."

What if your spouse told you they would give up their relationships with half of their present or former lovers to marry you? Would that satisfy you? Of course it wouldn't, and it shouldn't.

You want 100 percent loyalty from your spouse.

You want their all.

You want their best. Should Christ get less?

Years ago, I attended a funeral for someone I didn't know well. The preacher's sermon was highly complimentary. He described the deceased as a wonderful Christian. After the memorial service, I stood in the church yard with other mourners and overheard two men discussing the departed. One who had worked with the man for years and knew him well, said, "I never knew he was a Christian?"

What an indictment!

What if that was you? Would your friends call you a Christian? Do you do your best? Do you live a holy life? Do you read your Bible? Do you witness? Do you pray? Without ceasing? Doing your best costs something!

What kind of church member are you? Do you support your pastor? Do you attend every service? Do you give generously? Do you attend prayer meetings? Do you volunteer for Christian service as the need arises? Do you give your time? Can you honestly say you are doing your best if you don't?

My first pastorate was a small church in Tennessee. I was very young and very green and it was definitely a challenge. One man in the congregation didn't like me that well. He thought, among other things, that I preached too loud. "Why don't you just talk to us?" he would complain. He wasn't a real trouble maker, just the quintessential dissatisfied pew warmer.

Once in the middle of the night I got a call from this man. He was weeping so hard I could barely understand what he was saying. This was extremely out of character for a man who was normally without emotion. He asked me to come to his house right away. I had no idea what was wrong. I prayed earnestly as I drove. My assumption was that someone in the family was very sick or had died. He was indescribably upset on the phone.

When I arrived at the house, he was still crying, almost uncontrollably. I found the reason for his consternation was a dream—a dream about me. In his dream, he was watching me on an operating table and the surgeon was about to amputate my leg. He argued with the surgeon, saying he couldn't do this, I was too young. Then the surgeon turning to him and giving him the scalpel said, "You do it!"

The man cried and said, "I can't! I can't"

The surgeon responded, "You already have. You won't give him a leg to stand on." The man woke up in a cold sweat. I don't know that I have ever seen a man so frightened by a dream. After that night he was a changed man. He no longer complained. He was faithful to the church. He gave his money. He gave his time. He worked around the church. He did his best.

Are you doing your best?

Tozer wrote, "Refuse to be average. Let your heart soar as high as it will." No one would call him average. He wrote more than forty books, giving the lion's share of his royalties to the needy. His gravestone is simply but profoundly marked, "A. W. Tozer—Man of God." He did his best.

John Wesley, the founder of Methodism, gave God his best. He traveled more than 250,000 miles on horseback and preached 40,000 sermons. Well past eighty-five years of age, Wesley wrote on January 1, 1790, "I am now an old man, decayed from head to foot. My eyes are dim; my right hand shakes much; my mouth is hot and dry every morning; I have a lingering fever almost every day; my motion is weak and slow. However, blessed be God, I do not slack my labor; I can preach and write still." These are the words of a man who was giving God his best.

Wesley received thousands of dollars from the sale of the myriad of books he wrote. He kept very little for himself. Wesley died full of peace and joy at the ripe old age of eighty-seven. His estate consisted only of a worn clergy robe and his ministerial library. His real legacy, however, was the 541 ministers and 135,000 members of the Methodist church. He gave his best.

D. L. Moody was one of the greatest soul winners that ever lived. Early in his career, Moody met British revivalist Henry Varley in Dublin. Varley challenged the American evangelist with these words, "Moody, the world has yet to see what God can do with a man fully consecrated to Him." As Moody sailed back to America he said every plank on the deck of the ship seemed to have those words engraved on them. In Chicago Moody said the same words seemed to be written on every stone of the paved streets. Moody was determined to be that man. He consecrated his entire life to God. He gave Him his best. Moody changed his world.

What could we do today if we gave God our best?

What if you gave Him your best? Would it cost you something? Of course it would. Wouldn't it be worth whatever it cost?

Per Akvist, a Swedish missionary stood on the platform of a great crusade in Ethiopia. Like many times before, tens of thousands stood before him eager to hear the word of God. An old pastor was there and he was allowed to speak. He told of being a Christian minister under the heavy hand of communist rule in Ethiopia. The communist leaders had brought him to that very field many years before. With him were ten of the best men from his congregation; young men with friends and families; young believers that loved Jesus; young lives with unexplored potential. The men were bound and placed in a line before him and then the authorities demanded that he deny Christ. How could he deny the one who died for him?

When the pastor refused, the Marxist police went down the line and one at a time shot each of his young members in the head, killing them all. There is no question, they gave their best. It cost them their lives. What did it cost you this week?

Are you doing your best? Are you doing everything that you do for Christ with all your might? Are you giving your "supreme effort?"

If not, why not? Are you afraid it will cost too much? Jesus gave His best—He gave His all.

Most of us know Jimmy Carter as the former president of the United States, but Carter also had a distinguished military career. He was a graduate of the United States Naval Academy and during the second world war Carter bravely served on surface ships and submarines in both the Atlantic and Pacific fleets. When Admiral Hyman Rickover (then a captain) was carefully choosing a team for the Navy's nuclear submarine program he chose Lieutenant Carter. Carter became a nuclear engineer under Rickover's tutelage. The older sailor became a mentor to Carter who later stated Rickover's positive influence on his life was second only to that of his parents. In his autobiography, Carter told of his first interview with Rickover who was known for being abrasive and demanding. The admiral asked Carter about his rank in his class at the Naval Academy. Carter proudly answered, "Sir, I graduated 59th out of a class of 820." Carter waited for a congratulation that never came. Rickover was not impressed by the good standing. In response he asked a piercing question, "Did you always do your best?"

Initially Carter wanted to say "yes," but after giving it some thought he reluctantly admitted that he had not always done his best. Rickover stared coldly at the young lieutenant for a long time and then turned his chair around to end the interview. But before Carter could exit he replied with two haunting words that changed Carter's life, "Why not?"

Some day every believer will stand before their Savior to give account of their lives (Romans 14:12). Each man and woman will have to give a defense of how they spent their life in Christ. When you stand before Him, what if He asks, "Did you do your best?"

What will you say? Can you honestly answer, "Yes?"

If you can't say "yes," what if He raises His hands, exposing the ugly scars from the Roman nails and asks you, "Why not?"

And as Moses lifted up the serpent in the wilderness, even so must the Son of man be lifted up: That whosoever believeth in him should not perish, but have eternal life.

John 3:14

A SENSITIVE CHURCH

Centuries ago someone asked Martin Luther to recommend a book to him that was both agreeable and useful. "Agreeable and useful!" replied Luther. "Such a question is beyond my ability. The better things are the less they please."

Now, Christians seem to be looking for churches that are agreeable and useful—or perhaps not even useful—as long as they are agreeable. Manipulating members have made people pleasing the most prominent plank in many church's platform.

Often it seems churches in the western world are more anxious to mimic pop psychology than New Testament Christianity. Riding the latest wave, ministers no longer want to be called "pastors" and "evangelists." They prefer the ambiguous title of "life coaches"—whatever that is supposed to mean.

In this milieu of cultural relevance and religious correctness there are a couple of phrases that gained prominence in the 1990's—"user friendly" and "seeker sensitive"—and continue to dominate the church ethos.

Simply put, the idea is that going to church should be like a pleasant shopping experience. Large retailers have grown into colossal chains by learning a few tricks that make customers feel more at home in their stores. Churches are now trying to mimic their success. Obsolete sermonizing is being replaced by monologues, dialogue and dramas. Hymns have been replaced by contemporary choruses or even secular songs. In some cases, crosses have been stripped from church campuses because non-Christians may feel they are offensive.

It costs very little or perhaps nothing to be part of a user friendly church. It is trendy today to accept the unconverted as church members with the hopes of reaching them after they are on the church rolls.

One large Christian denomination announced their new attitude toward false religions was conversation, not conversion. Saying that Muslims and Buddhists are "lost" is a little too extreme for today's pablum-peddling pulpits.

Haven't Full Gospel churches reached a similar truce with non-Pentecostal evangelicals? There was a time when Pentecostals were despised as they told their Christian neighbors that God had given them something "more" in the baptism in the Holy Ghost. Now Pentecostals down play speaking in tongues and the Holy Ghost to be more acceptable and respectable to the larger church world.

Being at peace with other faiths is quite popular today. It wasn't always this way. J. C. Ryle, a nineteenth century evangelical leader in the Church of England said, "Let us never be guilty of sacrificing any portion of truth on the altar of peace."

What are we sacrificing for "peace" today?

A Pentecostal church was experiencing the initial stages of Holy Ghost revival with the accompanying physical manifestations of God's presence. When a few parishioners began to complain, the pastor became alarmed and announced, "We will not allow anything to go in this church that offends visitors."

God was not "user friendly" enough.

I wonder if Jesus could have preached there? No. I do not wonder. I know He could not.

Can you imagine Jesus visiting a church today? What if a blind man came for healing? What if He spit in a potted plant, made mud with His own spit and put it on the blind man's eyes. It would matter little that the man was healed . . . Jesus' crude and divisive style wouldn't fit into the cookie-cutting mold of modern "churchianity." A mud-making Messiah would offend today's church as much as He offended His religious contemporaries in the first century.

Do you think Herod was offended when Jesus derogatorily referred to him as a fox?

Do you think the Pharisees were offended when He called them snakes?

How about the money changers that He drove from the Temple with a whip? Do you think they went on their way saying, "I love this church, Pastor Jesus is so friendly and his approach is so relevant." Not likely! There is a better chance that they were offended by Him—deeply offended.

What about when Annanias and Saphira dropped dead in church, struck down by God for lying to the Holy Ghost? Do you think any guests were offended that day? That was God's idea of Sunday morning drama. The Bible says "great fear came upon all the church" (Acts 5:11).

English pastor and prolific author, F. B. Myer, once said, "Between such irreconcilable opposites as the church and the world, *there cannot be but antagonism and strife*. Each treasures and seeks what the other rejects as worthless. Each is devoted to ends that are inimical to the dearest interests of the other."

This is not to say that a church shouldn't be cognizant of the needs of both members and guests. Of course, the church should facilitate worship by providing a comfortable, clean and convenient environment. But, how far should a church go to be non-offensive to unbelievers? Jesus said His followers would be "hated" of all men for the sake of His name (Matthew 10:22). He said

He didn't come to bring peace on the earth but a sword (Matthew 10:34).

That does not sound very "user friendly." While today's church seeks to be attractive to the world and popular with unbelievers, Jesus said, "Woe unto you, when all men shall speak well of you!" (Luke 6:26).

Luther said, "Always preach in such a way that if the people listening do not come to hate their sin, they will instead hate you." How do you sell that point of view to our user-friendly ministries that had rather entertain politicians and coddle television talk show hosts than please the God of heaven?

Baptist pastor and theologian Alexander Maclaren correctly noted, "The measure of our discord with the world is the measure of our accord with the saviour."

"Why in God's name do you expect to be accepted everywhere?" Ravenhill asks. "How is it the world couldn't get on with the holiest man that ever lived, and it can get on with you and me?"

The fact is, the church of the New Testament was not a seeker sensitive church. How can a church be both seeker sensitive and New Testament today?

The church of the first century *was* a Spirit sensitive church!

In 1 Thessalonians 5:19, Paul said, "Quench not the Spirit." Yet, many churches, even Pentecostal and Charismatic churches make no room for the Holy Spirit.

"If the Holy Spirit was withdrawn from the church today, ninety-five percent of what we do would go on and no one would know the difference," wrote Tozer. "If the Holy Spirit had been withdrawn from the New Testament church, ninety-five percent of what they did would stop, and everybody would know the difference."

Those who are familiar with doves report that they are a timid, almost anxious bird. They are seldom aggressive and must be treated delicately. This is why the world has chosen the dove to be a symbol for peace. It is also why the dove so appropriately symbolizes the Holy Spirit.

Church leaders must be sensitive to the Holy Spirit. The heavenly dove must not fly. There is no worse fate for a church.

Being an itinerate minister for many years, I have had many and varied experiences. One I will never forget happened at an Assemblies of God church in South Carolina. I preached on the baptism in the Holy Spirit and speaking in tongues. The next morning I got a phone call from a very angry pastor. He wanted to meet me for breakfast. As a guest speaker, the last thing you want to do is have the pastor upset with you, so obviously his tone concerned me. On my way to the restaurant, I racked my brain, trying to think of what I might have done or said.

The answer shocked me.

He was upset because I had preached that speaking in tongues was the evidence of the Holy Ghost baptism. Although "Pentecostal" in name, the church had assimilated a number of non-Pentecostals and to accommodate them he had taught his people that they didn't need to manifest a prayer language when baptized in the Holy Ghost. The same pastor rebuked members of his church when they yielded to physical manifestations of the Holy Spirit. I felt the Holy Spirit was grieved. This pastor was sensitive to the non-Pentecostals in his congregation, but he was not Spirit sensitive.

To illustrate the absurdity of this, only a few weeks before I had preached the very same sermon in a Southern Baptist church where many were baptized in the Holy Ghost. These precious Baptist people, hungry for the Holy Spirit filled the altars singing:

They were in an upper chamber
They were all in one accord
When the Holy Ghost descended
As was promised by our Lord.

A Spirit sensitive church will not quench the Holy Spirit.

A Spirit sensitive church will not merely tolerate the Holy Spirit and His manifestations; a Spirit sensitive church will celebrate the Holy Spirit and His manifestations.

A Spirit sensitive church will welcome the Holy Spirit. A Spirit sensitive church will pray, "Come Holy Spirit, Come." In a Spirit sensitive church the Holy Spirit can do anything He wants, with anyone He wants, anytime He wants, and in any way He wants.

When the Holy Spirit fell on the day of Pentecost, Peter proudly announced, "This is that!" Thousands were saved and baptized in the Holy Spirit. The church grew exponentially. Wherever they preached, Christ was exalted, the Holy Spirit was poured out and there were supernatural signs and wonders.

They were Spirit sensitive.

Many churches advertise to have the same thing today. They should take another look at the book of Acts. *This is not that!* What your church has may be good, but it isn't that. It isn't even close to that! Only those who have never tasted "that" could think that what we have today is what they had in the New Testament.

In fact, as long as a church is satisfied with "this" it will never have "that."

I am the youngest of four children. My sister married when I was only six. We adopted our youngest daughter when I was almost 35, so my sister has grandchildren older than my daughter. For years we all had Christmas together at our parents' home. As my siblings had children and then grandchildren it was a blast. There was always a crowded house, loads of gifts, tons of food and the laughter of many children. As their families grew, my sister's children wanted to have their own family Christmas and eventually with the passing of our parents, each of us went our own way, forming our own traditions.

There was one problem. Our daughter came last among the children and she missed out on the great Christmas bash. She has heard us talk about how much fun it was to have a huge crowd of family together at the home place with gifts for everyone and from everyone—but she never experienced it.

How many young people in churches today have never experienced a real Pentecostal outpouring? They hear talk of Azusa Street. They hear of revivals, but many have never been part of one. They hear others talk of what the Holy Spirit can do, but they have never seen it for themselves. In their church the Holy Spirit is ignored. If He makes an appearance, He is shuffled away to a back room. Guests might not understand if He is allowed to move in the main auditorium. They might be offended. No wonder this generation feels cheated. No wonder they are leaving the church. No wonder Pentecostal denominations are in decline.

The New Testament church must be Spirit sensitive.

The New Testament church was also sin sensitive.

Sin is a word seldom heard in modern churches. Many believe it belongs in antique shops with kerosene lanterns, potbelly stoves, wagon wheels and Kewpie dolls.

In the past twenty years, there has been a "dumbing down" of the church. It does not take much discernment to recognize it is the work of satan to destroy the effectiveness of kingdom work. One of the tricks in the devil's tool box is to label all preaching against sin as "legalism" or "condemnation."

Jesus, who told the adulterous woman, "Neither do I condemn thee," also told her to "go and sin no more."

Many pulpits today are offering boatloads of "neither do I condemn thee" but only drops of "go and sin no more" (John 8:11).

Paul said, "Awake to righteousness, and sin not" (1 Corinthians 15:34). He didn't say sin a lot. He didn't say sin a little. He said "sin not."

The Bible is clear, "The soul that sinneth, it shall die" (Ezekiel 18:4).

A New Testament church will still believe that sin is sin. A New Testament pastor will not be afraid to preach about it.

One New Testament word for sin is to "miss the mark." Paul used this word in Romans 3:23, "All have sinned . . ." The idea is of an archer aiming for the bull's eye. He may hit the target, but if he misses the bull's eye, he missed the mark. Not to hit the mark is sin. Doing wrong things is a sin. Failing to do right things is a sin. It is missing the mark.

It costs something to hit the mark. It costs something to even aim for the mark. A user-friendly faith costs little or nothing. Real Christianity costs everything.

The New Testament held a high standard for membership. When a Corinthian fornicator was unrepentant, Paul said he should be put out of the church and "delivered to satan" (1 Corinthians 5:5). Throughout history, New Testament churches have demanded separation from the world and sin. Early Pentecostals were no exception. They were known as "holiness" people.

Today, their spiritual heirs host poker runs and gambling tournaments in bars to "reach the lost." Pastors spice their sermons with profanity to be relevant. Church motorcycle rallies provide secular entertainment by heathen bands and close their eyes to alcohol and drug abuse on church property, all in the name of evangelism. Who is it that really needs the evangelist? Is it the church or the world? Is anything a sin today?

As this book is being prepared for press, an Assemblies of God congregation in Springfield, Missouri has partnered with a tattoo artist to provide free body art to its members after a Sunday service. Advertised as a means to raise money for a children's charity, the campus pastor and his staff were among the first to get in line for the permanent inking.

This nonsense was taking place within spitting distance of the international headquarters of this once "Holiness" denomination. Was there an outcry from the leadership of the movement? Of course not. Quite to the contrary, the General Superintendent, speaking for the entire executive team, defended the event saying most of the tattoos were "faith based." He even suggested that what was happening at the church was similar in the minds of some to the scars in and on Paul's body, saying, for some young believers today "tattoos are not a sign of paganism as condemned in Leviticus, but a way to bear in their body the marks of Christ."

Bazarre! Read 2 Corinthians 11:21-28. Think about all that Paul suffered. How could anyone in Christian leadership allow the godly, self-sacrificing experiences of Paul to be compared with a worldly, self-satisfying fad without a personal protest?

Is anything a sin today?

Over and over again at the Brownsville Revival in Pensacola, Florida, Evangelist Steve Hill told the audience, "Sin is doing anything Jesus wouldn't do." Watching things on television that Jesus wouldn't watch is a sin. Telling or listening to jokes Jesus wouldn't tell is a sin. Using language Jesus wouldn't use is a sin. Going to places where Jesus wouldn't go is a sin. Marking, cutting and piercing your body in ways Jesus wouldn't is a sin.

That is too high a standard for a seeker sensitive Christian, but it is the only standard for a sin sensitive Christian.

The New Testament church was also a souls sensitive church.

D. L. Moody was one of the greatest soul winners that ever lived. He not only reached thousands through mass evangelism events, he also was a tireless personal evangelist, individually witnessing to someone every day.

When Moody was asked why he was so driven to reach the lost, he said that when he was converted that God showed him the world was an ocean and everyone in it was drowning. God gave Moody a lifeboat and said, "'Save as many as you can." D. L. Moody was souls-sensitive.

A number of years ago while in prayer, I saw a very graphic image of our world going to hell. I hesitate to say that what I saw was a vision, that terminology is too often abused. What I can say is that the living pictures that I saw touched me profoundly and gave me dramatic new insights into the world harvest. I felt impressed to write them down at the time and I pray they will also touch you.

What I saw was a bird's eye view of our world as it must look to God. I wish that I was an artist so that I could put what I saw on canvas. But, since God did not give me that ability, I will attempt to draw the picture with words.

I saw a large plateau which represented the church. What was happening on this elevated plain is very important, but I will describe it later.

About eight or nine feet beneath the mesa there was a huge declining field crowded with millions of people—people of all races and nationalities. The variety of costumes testified to the diversity of the crowd. The rich and the poor were there. There were both young people and older adults in the multitude, but oddly enough, I saw no children.

Almost as far as the eye could see, men and women were pressed together like a living, breathing collage of humanity. It was obvious to me that I was seeing the lost world. At the extremes of this vast expanse I saw the awful fire and smoke of eternal damnation. The inferno was creeping slowly forward and it's destructive flames reached further into the crowd like the tentacles of a fiery octopus.

Hopeless thousands were being pulled into the burning pit.

Anxiety seems like an understatement as I still see the faces of the multitude. They looked at the fire and then at the safety of the church, high on the plateau above the threat of the flames. Those close to the ledge were trying desperately to climb out of the pit, but the wall was too high. They were perishing!

As disturbing as this picture may seem, what I saw on the upper plane was more alarming. I saw the church going about its normal activities, mostly oblivious to the cries of the perishing. One portly fellow with a bib around his neck was sitting at a well provisioned table eating a large drumstick. He smiled with pleasure as he enjoyed his feast. Another man was quietly reading his Bible, occasionally looking over his shoulder into the pit as if he was annoyed that the cries of the crowd were disturbing his devotions.

Another group of church members were singing and dancing. Joining their arms together, they danced about in a circle that brought them to the very edge of the mesa. They were so enthralled with their celebration of Christ, they didn't even notice the unfortunates that were slipping into Hell's eternal torment.

Two men that I saw were angrily shouting at each other as each pointed a hostile finger in the other's face. I could not hear what these Christians were arguing about, but my experience tells me that it was probably something of extreme importance like whether to sing hymns or choruses or perhaps even the weightier matter of sanctuary carpet color. They too were so caught up in what they were doing they couldn't see their own friends and family that were getting closer and closer to the pit.

Next to the edge of the plateau, a man wearing a clerical collar was throwing papers to the crowd below. On each paper was written only two words, "Church Membership." Those who could reach one of the certificates were thrilled. Their countenances were changed from desperation to hope as they lifted the paper over their head. How sad it was to watch their feigned faith quickly fade as the fingers of fire reached up from the pit and literally incinerated the papers, causing them to vanish from their uplifted hands.

In the midst of all this foolishness, there was one lone man that caught both my attention and my admiration. He was kneeling at the edge of the plateau. With his sleeves rolled up, he was reaching down into the lower plane and working feverishly to pull as many of the lost out of the pit as was humanly possible.

Next to this gospel worker was a tall cross. He held tenaciously to the cross with one hand while he rescued the perishing with the other. It was such a beautiful picture, if he hadn't had the cross as an anchor, the panic-stricken masses might have pulled him into perdition. But as long as he clung tightly to the cross, his footing was secure. His anchor held.

As I saw this shocking panorama, Luke 10:2 come to my mind, "The harvest truly is great, but the labourers are few: pray ye therefore the Lord of the harvest, that he would send forth labourers into his harvest." Although I had preached from the text many times, it never meant more to me than at this moment.

I saw the Lord's church feeding themselves physically and spiritually, singing, dancing, and even quarreling while the multitudes were slipping into hell. I saw the church offering false hope to a world that needed real help. I also saw one faithful laborer snatching as many as he could from the burning. Yet, as willing as he was and as hard as he worked, there was no way that he could rescue more than a few. The harvest was too great!

The harvest is even greater today. America, indeed, the whole world needs a souls sensitive church.

Finally, the New Testament was a Savior sensitive church.

Jesus said, "And I, if I be lifted up from the earth, will draw all men unto me" (John 12:32). A New Testament church exalts Jesus Christ.

Churches that exalt personalities will fail. Churches that exalt programs will fail. They might excel at multiplying buildings, bodies and bucks, but they have failed at the only purpose for which they were created.

A church that exalts Jesus is never a failure.

Jesus said I am the truth—all other religions and belief systems are a lie, leading men to an eternal hell (John 14.6).

He said I am life—all others offer spiritual death (John 11:12; 14:6).

He said I am the way—man cannot find God except by following the path He offers (John 14:6). All other paths, no matter how well intentioned, have destruction as a destination. There are ways that seem right to men, but they lead to death (Proverbs 14:12).

He said I am the door—you cannot get to God except by passing through Him (John 10:9).

He said I am the living bread —nothing else can satisfy a hungry soul (John 6:51).

He said I am the Alpha and Omega, the beginning and the end, the first and the last—redemption for humankind starts in Him and is completed in Him (Revelation 1:8; 22:13). He is the "author and finisher of our faith" (Hebrews 12:2).

He said I am the light of the world—those who do not follow Him are living in darkness (John 8:12).

He said I am the good shepherd—He gave His life for His sheep (John 1 0: 11).

He said I am the root and offspring of David—as God He was David's creator, as man He is the heir to His kingdom (Revelation 22:16).

He said I am the true vine—those who stay connected to Him will bear much fruit (John 15: 1).

He said I am the resurrection—He was the first raised from the dead and the hope of all who die in Him (John 11:25).

He said I am the bright and morning star—He is the brilliant hope that shines with the dawning of each new day (Revelation 22:16).

He said, I am He that liveth, and was dead; and, behold, I am alive for evermore. He said He held the keys of hell and of death (Revelation 1:18). Only Jesus conquered death and the grave, becoming the first fruits for all believers to follow.

He said I am the Son of God—no one else can rightly make that claim (John 10:36). His name is above every name. Jesus must be exalted!

He said if I be lifted up, I will draw all men unto Me. Espresso and cappuccino machines, playgrounds, rock bands, fog machines and strobe lights may draw a crowd, but when Jesus is lifted up, men are drawn to Him and to His offer of eternal life.

He is not an answer—He is *the* answer, the only answer.

A New Testament church must be sensitive—not to the whims of man; not to the fickle fads of an ever evolving popular culture—but to Him, the never changing Savior of the world. Contemporary churches who are always jumping through perpetual hoops to accommodate unconverted or unsanctified men may find the only one they have offended is God—the one that must never be offended.

Almost four hundred years ago, the Puritan Thomas Adams said it well, "No man more truly loves God than he that is most fearful to offend *Him.*"

But Jehoiada waxed old, and was full of days when he died, an hundred and thirty years old was he when he died. And they buried him in the city of David among the kings, because he had done good in Israel, both toward God, and toward his house. Now after the death of Jehoiada came the princes of Judah, and made obeisance to the king. Then the king hearkened unto them. And they left the house of the LORD God of their fathers, and served groves and idols: and wrath come upon Judah and Jerusalem for this their trespass.

2 Chronicles 24:15-18

WHEN JEHOIADA DIED

During the Old Testament period of the kings, the Jewish kingdom was divided between two competing monarchies. The southern division was ruled by the kings of Judah while the ten northern tribes were ruled by the kings of Israel.

In the mid-ninth century B.C. Judah experienced the brief reign of a wicked king named Ahaziah. Ahaziah's mother was Athaliah, the daughter of Jezebel and Ahab. This despotic duo were the worst of Israel's often wicked and ungodly sovereigns.

Athaliah the daughter of the king of Israel had married Jehoram the son of Jehosaphat, king of Judah, in an attempt to bring the two kingdom's together. This significantly enhanced her kingdom and her clout.

Athaliah's son, King Ahaziah, was killed and her delicate position was threatened. If one of Ahaziah's sons ascended to the throne, the ambitious and conniving Athaliah might no longer hold her coveted position as queen mother. In an almost unimaginable grasp for power she cruelly ordered the death of all the royal family including her own grandchildren.

Her every competitor, every descendent of David was slain—no, wait, not every one. God had made a promise that an heir of David would always sit on the throne. Joash, an infant child of Ahaziah, was secreted away by his aunt and concealed from his brutal grandmother. Try as they may, men cannot prevent the will and plan of God. His plans always trump the schemes of man.

Athaliah reigned for six years. All this time, unknown to the wicked queen, little Joash was hidden away in the Temple by his uncle, an old priest named Jehoiada.

A godly man, Jehoiada, spent years devising a plan to put Joash on the throne. He assembled a company of priests from throughout the country. The throng was armed with weapons kept in the Temple since the reign of David. They surrounded the young boy with priestly guards and then crowned him as king. As the crowd witnessed the coronation, they cried "God save the King" and rejoiced. Trumpets were sounded, musicians played and the Temple choir sang praises to God.

When Athaliah heard the uproar of the people she ran into the Temple, tearing her clothes and crying "Treason! Treason!" It was too late, Joash was the new king. The priests followed her out of the Temple and put her to death with a sword. The season of grief visited on Israel by Ahab, Jezebel and their seed had finally ended.

Conditions improved dramatically during Joash's period of influence. Idol worship ceased. The house of Baal was torn down. Temple worship was restored. Animal sacrifices were offered to God. The Law of Moses was read and obeyed. The Bible says, "All the people rejoiced." It was a wonderful season.

The Temple had fallen into disrepair under the wicked sovereigns and instruments of worship had been offered to Baal. This was a matter of great concern for Joash and Jehoiada. The king placed a chest outside the gate of the Temple and ordered the people to bring their tithes and offerings as Moses had taught them. Daily they emptied the chest until they had accumulated an "abundance" of money. The Temple was repaired, strengthened and refurnished. These were the best of times.

But then Jehoiada grew old. God gave him a long and prosperous life, but at one-hundred and thirty years of age he died. The godly priest was so loved and respected they buried him with the kings.

Jehoiada had barely passed from the scene when the princes of Judah began to influence Joash. First they flattered him. Then they began to complain against Jehoiada. "Listen," they murmured, "the old man was too strict on us. The old ways were just legalism and bondage. Let us go out and worship outside of the city." Idolatry was their intention. Joash tolerated their compromise and in a very short time they had returned to the evil ways of their fathers. There was no difference between them and their heathen neighbors.

They built groves to venerate idols and worshipped Baal and Asherah, the gods of their heathen neighbors. Baal was the god of the sun, their provider god. Asherah was the goddess of sensual pleasure.

The very nature and description of these two false gods are an illustration of why God loathes idolatry. When His people look to idols they don't trust Him for their provision and they give themselves to entertainments and pleasures that gratify the flesh.

God was angry.

He sent a number of prophets—Elisha, Micah, and others. The people would give no ear to them. Even Joash hardened his heart to God. Without the tutelage of godly Jehoiada he had lost his way.

Then God sent the Prophet Zechariah. He was the son of Jehoiada, the king's beloved protector and mentor. He had the same message as his revered father. "Ye hath forsaken the Lord and He hath forsaken you." Surely, Joash would hear Zechariah. Surely, he would lead the nation back to the God of his youth.

Did Joash receive Zechariah? No. Just the opposite occurred. The king had him stoned. He should have stoned the idolators that were destroying his kingdom, but he killed the godly messenger, the son of his own rescuer and mentor. How quickly Israel had fallen.

God would allow no more. Soon, judgment came. A small army of Syrians violently struck, ransacked and plundered Judah. Their attack left Joash weak and sick and his servants came and killed him in his own bed. Defeated and disgraced he wasn't even buried with the kings.

Think about it, Jehoiada, the priest, led the people toward God and he was buried like a king; Joash, the king, led the people away from God and he was layed to rest in disgrace.

There is a modern parallel to this narrative. It is not a "type" in the biblical sense, just an illustration for comparison.

In many ways, Jehoiada is like the Pentecostal pioneers at the beginning of the twentieth century. God used them to restore the power and principles of the kingdom—much of which had been lost since the second century.

These Pentecostal trailblazers preached the baptism in the Holy Spirit with the accompanying evidence of speaking with other tongues. They were ostracized for their peculiar belief, but they were uncompromising in declaring that the book of Acts was still true. They sought the approval of no man. God was with them. Their success was without parallel. From brush arbors, storefronts and back-side-of-the-tracks buildings they preached and prospered. God was with them.

They preached divine healing and God honored His word with miracles and signs following. They had faith for the incredible and when they prayed and believed the impossible become possible.

Pentecostal patriarchs preached and practiced separation from the world. They dressed modestly and avoided secular amusements and entertainments. They were not ashamed to be called "Holiness." Did some of them go too far? Perhaps, but they believed that extremism in the pursuit of God was no vice. Or, as Harry Ironside put it, "No one ever lost out by excessive devotion to Christ."

While hating sin, they promoted love and acceptance in a way the church world had seldom or never witnessed. When integration of the races was illegal in much of the country, blacks and whites worshipped together and prayed together at Pentecostal altars. Frank Bartleman attended the Azusa Street revival and proclaimed, "The color line was washed away in the blood."

These people denounced sectarianism. They were not Baptists, Methodists or Pentecostals. They were Christians. Even as they began to forge alliances for the promotion of the gospel their founding documents announced they would never become a denomination, but would always remain a loosely organized fellowship of believers and churches. Bartleman said, ". . .they will never consent to the present work turned into a sect. God's people are simply not going to be led into the snare of human organization again."

These people were worshippers—exuberant worshippers. It was their enthusiasm that drew many to their meetings. They sang loud and long. They prayed. Oh, how they prayed. Their prayers rattled the windows; more important, they shook the heavens. They shouted, they jumped, they danced. They lifted their voices and their hands to a God who loved them, saved them and filled them with the Holy Ghost. When appropriate, they sat quietly in His awesome presence. They wept. A. G. Osterberg said the Azusa Street revival began in tears and lived in tears.

This, too, was a wonderful season of God's blessings. Some would say it was the best of times.

But, time marches on. Soon these old pioneers began to leave the stage. One by one they were gone. A new generation came . . . and then another. Then, the princes of Judah came.

In the Pentecostal movement, the princes have a name—respectability and acceptability. Curse these words!

There lies within the heart of man a desire to be accepted and respected by his peers. Nothing is more crippling to a revivalistic movement. Jesus said, "Beware when all men speak well of you, so did their fathers to the false prophets" (Luke 6:26). And yet, the approval of men, especially religious men, seems to be the principal goal of many Pentecostal leaders and churches.

James wrote, "Know ye not that friendship with the world is enmity with God?" (James 4:4). The church forgets what the great evangelist, Gipsy Smith knew all too well, "If you're really in with God, you'll be at odds with the world." It costs something to be different. Today, many Pentecostals believe it costs too much.

Like the princes of Judah a new generation of Pentecostals have started to complain.

"The old ways were too extreme."

"Those Pentecostal fathers were too legalistic."

"We will never be respectable if we carry on like this. Do we really need all this emotion? It is time to tune it down and turn it off."

"Look, this separation message is just legalism and condemnation."

"Is speaking in tongues really necessary? It is so controversial and it offends our evangelical brethren."

Without realizing how far from the path they have strayed, the church begins to go after false gods. What did Baal and Asherah represent?

A failure to trust God as the only source and sensual pleasure.

If a church becomes reliant on man-made, seeker sensitive, and user friendly programs and devices is it really trusting God? In a recent seminar on church growth the speakers discussed cutting edge technology, usher and greeter training, entertainments, amusements and a dozen other things. Prayer was never mentioned. God barely was. It was if He was irrelevant. Young pastors are being taught how to build churches without God's help. What are they building?

Are we worshipping the idols of self-reliance and pleasure?

Countless Pentecostal church are no different from the denominational church across the street or down the road. Sadly, this is often by design. Secular music that was once a taboo entertainment is now part of "worship."

Rock legend Jerry Lee Lewis was raised in a Pentecostal home and attended an Assemblies of God Bible school. According to one unconfirmed story he was dismissed from the school after one of his performances was a bit too "worldly." Years later, it is reported that the president of the student body caught up with Lewis and asked him if he was still playing the devil's music. Lewis's alleged answer was as intuitive as it was convicting, "Yes, I am. But you know it's strange, the same music they kicked me out of school for is the same music they play in their churches today. The difference is, I know I am playing for the devil and they don't." God help us, the world can see while the church is blind! This is spiritual insanity.

A. B. Simpson, founder of the Christian and Missionary Alliance warned his generation, "The chief danger of the church today is that it is trying to get on the same side as the world, instead of turning the world upside down. Our Master expects us to accomplish results, even if they bring opposition and conflict. Anything is better than compromise, apathy, and paralysis. God, give to us an intense cry for the old-time power of the Gospel and the Holy Ghost."

The Holy Spirit is seldom welcomed in many if not most Pentecostal churches. If He tries to move, He is sent to a back room. Pentecostal extremism, it is believed, is neither acceptable nor respectable and these are the gods many now serve.

"Pentecostal" people now move from "Spirit-filled" churches to other evangelical churches without noticing a difference. They are not sufficiently grounded in the Bible to realize that in so doing they are accepting doctrines their spiritual predecessors found damnable. Their fathers and mothers left those same churches fifty and a hundred years ago because the truth of Pentecost was radically different!

In many Pentecostal churches one third or less of the congregants have received the baptism in the Holy Spirit with evidentiary tongues. Are they really Pentecostal churches? When do they cease to be Pentecostal? When *no one* speaks in tongues? Is this why many Pentecostal churches are stagnant or in decline? It costs something to have revival. Not to have revival may cost even more.

A major Pentecostal denomination recently announced a conference to raise up "a new generation of Pentecostals." The keynote speaker for the event was a non-Pentecostal!

Have we lost our minds?

Does anyone see what is happening? Is there no prophetic voice? Someone, anyone, please climb to the roof top and shout it to the top of your voice! Let's destroy the false gods of pleasure. They are surely destroying us!

The Pentecostal movement needs some modern-day Zechariahs to preach the same message their fathers preached. Pentecostalism needs a wake-up call.

How will the movement respond? It is clear, many do not want to go back. It costs too much. They have worshipped at the altars of respectability and acceptability for too long. Some will continue to close their ears to the message that brought life and blessing to the movement in the beginning. Some of the worst critics of real Pentecostal revival are now in "Pentecostal" churches.

To ignore the call to repent and return is to face spiritual death. Church history is cluttered with the dry bones of way too many great revival movements that lost their way and never came back.

Is it even possible to come back?

Frank Bartleman wrote, "No religious body has ever recovered itself after its 'first love' was lost." Certainly decline is easier than recovery. Any Bible student can trace the fall of the Ephesian church from the Acts of the Apostles to the Book of Ephesians and finally to a backslidden church in Revelation.

God is patient, but He will not tolerate backsliding forever. Candlesticks can and will be removed.

Some will stone the prophets. They always have. They always will.

Some, however, will have the courage to face the Baal worshippers. They will repent and restore the faith of our fathers. For them, Pentecost will be Pentecost again. The princes of respectability will wail.

So be it, let them wail.

Faithful, uncompromising saints will pay the price? Will you be one of them?

God will have a people. He always has. He always will. Our God reigns!

And it come to pass, as they still went on, and talked, that, behold, there appeared a chariot of fire, and horses of fire, and parted them both asunder; and Elijah went up by a whirlwind into heaven. And Elisha saw it, and he cried, My father, my father, the chariot of Israel, and the horsemen thereof. And he saw him no more: and he took hold of his own clothes, and rent them in two pieces. He took up also the mantle of Elijah that fell from him, and went back, and stood by the bank of Jordan; And he took the mantle of Elijah that fell from him, and smote the waters, and said, Where is the LORD God of Elijah? and when he also had smitten the waters, they parted hither and thither: and Elisha went over.

2 Kings 2:14

WHERE IS THE LORD GOD OF ELIJAH?

Who is this Lord God of Elijah?

The Bible says the Lord God of Elijah shut up the heavens that it did not rain for three and one-half years. Elijah walked in the palace of Israel's King Ahab and said "As the Lord liveth it isn't going to rain . . ." and it didn't rain, not even one drop for three years and six months.

Those who live in dry places know what it is to go without rain. North Texas and Western Oklahoma go through long periods of drought. The earth will crack open from the scorching sun and heat. Crops will wilt in the field and farmers are forced to sell their stock as ponds dry and watering holes vanish. That is after only several months without significant rain.

What if it didn't rain for three years? The conditions would be unbearable. Even in the ten years of the horrible Dust Bowl Era, precipitation was only fifteen to twenty-five percent less than normal. 1934, the worst year of all the rainfall was still just fifty percent less than the average for the region. There was never an extended time that it didn't rain at all, certainly never for three years.

Even the Atacama Desert in Chile, the driest place on the earth gets a few drops of rain every year.

On average Israel usually gets a little less than twenty-five inches of rain annually. For three years and six months they got no rain. Zero. Nada. Not a drop.

Why? Because the Lord God of Elijah shut up the heavens. He wanted to get the attention of Israel, and especially the wicked king. If He should choose, He could just as easily shut the heavens over America, Australia or Europe. The Lord God of Elijah is mighty! He is long suffering, but He won't be patient forever.

The Lord God of Elijah also sent fire down from Heaven. The false prophets of Baal and prophets of the grove were flourishing in a backslidden Israel. God was very displeased and called Elijah to confront the idolaters. He summoned all the prophets of Baal and prophets of the grove to a showdown.

According to Elijah's proposal, they would build two altars, one for God and one for Baal. They would pray for fire from heaven to consume their sacrifices. The God that answered by fire would be recognized as the only true and living God. Elijah was outnumbered eight hundred and fifty to one, but the odds were in His favor!

First, the false prophets built an altar, placed their sacrifice on it and prayed to their gods. When much emotion and enthusiasm by the idolaters created no results, Elijah began to mock them. It seems Elijah failed the contemporary course on non-offensive church.

"Cry louder, maybe your god is asleep."

"Maybe he is on a trip."

"Perhaps he is talking to someone else."

In a religious panic, they began to cry louder and cut their flesh with knives and spears. The Bible says, "There was neither voice, nor any to answer, nor any that regarded."

Now it was Elijah's turn. He repaired the altar of God. One can only guess why it was broken down, but a broken altar will never bring the fire.

Elijah placed a bullock on the altar. This, however, was not enough. Elijah wanted to shut the mouths of the skeptics forever. He dug a trench around his altar and then began to soak it in water. Twelve barrels of water were poured on the altar. The water "ran round about." The trench was filled with water. This would be no slight of hand. This would be no bogus magician's hoax. God would prove that He was God.

Elijah prayed a short prayer, less than seventy words in the English translation. There is a time to pray long. This was not the time.

The Bible says, "Then the fire of the Lord fell." What a simple but powerful statement. The fire consumed the sacrifice, it burned up the altar, including the stones and even the dust. The barrels of water in the trench instantly evaporated.

If the Israelites needed a confirmation, they had one. They fell on their faces and cried, "The Lord, He is God." At Elijah's command all the prophets of Baal were killed by the people.

In answer to the prophet's prayer, the Lord sent fire from heaven and demonstrated that He is the one and only living God. This is the Lord God of Elijah.

After the long crippling drought of three years and six months, the Lord God of Elijah sent rain on the earth.

Elijah knew it was time for the dry season to end. He told the king that he heard the sound of an abundance of rain. Believing it would rain was not enough. Elijah went high upon a mountain to pray.

Six times he sent his servant out to look for a physical confirmation that his prayers had been answered. Six times the servant returned to report there was no sign of rain. Elijah continued to pray. James said he prayed "effectually and fervently." The seventh time the servant was sent out. This time he returned with just a little hope. There was a small cloud arising from the sea, only the size of a man's hand. That was enough for Elijah. He believed; he prayed; now, he saw.

Elijah, anticipating a downpour, ran for the city of Jezreel. In his zeal, he overtook the chariot of the king. The skies become black with clouds and there was a "great" rain.

The same God that shut the heavens and dried the clouds for three and a half years, now opened the skies for a great rain. The Lord God of Elijah is a powerful God!

The Lord God of Elijah took his prophet to Heaven! Elijah and Elisha were walking along together. They knew something was coming. Suddenly, a chariot of fire with horses of fire separated them and Elijah was taken to heaven in a whirlwind.

As Elijah ascended, his mantle descended. Elisha picked up the mantle, struck the Jordan River crying, "Where is the Lord God of Elijah?" The same power present with Elijah divided the waters and Elisha crossed the Jordan on dry ground.

There is no God like the Lord God of Elijah!!

In these difficult times, the world needs the Lord God of Elijah. The unchurched, the idolaters, yes, even the church, needs to see His miraculous power displayed. Many believe it, some pray for it, and very few see it.

Where is the Lord God of Elijah?

Believe it or not, the answer is simple! He is right here! Right now!

The Psalmist wrote, "Whether shall I go from thy Spirit? or whither shall I flee from your presence? If I ascend up into heaven, thou art there: if I make my bed in hell, behold thou art there. If I take wind of the morning and dwell in the uttermost parts of the sea; Even there shall thy hand lead me and thy right hand shall hold me" (Psalm 139:7-10).

He is everywhere! He is omnipresent. He is right here.

"Now, wait just a minute," you may be tempted to say. It seems that something doesn't compute. If God is right here, right now, He must not like be like He was back then.

Wrong!

Scripture plainly says, "Jesus Christ the same yesterday, and to day, and forever" (Hebrews 13:8). In Malachi 3:6 the prophet writes, "For I am the Lord, I change not."

If this be true, and it most certainly is, then where are the demonstrations of His mighty power? Like Gideon of old, a new generation has reason to ask, "Oh my Lord, if the Lord be with us, why then is all this befallen us? and where be all his miracles which our fathers told us of . . ." (Judges 6:13).

Where is the Lord God of Elijah?

The difficulty is not in the answer to this question. The answer is true. He is here!

The problem is with the question itself. The wrong question is being asked. The real question is not "Where is the Lord God of Elijah?" We know where

He is. The question of the hour is "Where are the Elijahs of the Lord God?"

It is clear what the Lord God of Elijah is like and what He can do. But, what about Elijah, what kind of man was he?

Elijah was a man of prayer. James wrote "Elias was a man subject to like passions as we are, and he prayed earnestly that it might not rain: and it rained not on the earth by the space of three years and six months. And he prayed again and the heavens gave rain" (James 5:17).

If men today would pray like Elijah, they would see the results of Elijah. God still sends the fire of Pentecostal revival when men pray like Elijah prayed. God still sends the rain of His presence when men pray like Elijah prayed.

Speaking of the earliest days of the Pentecostal movement, Frank Bartleman said, "In the early Azusa days you could hardly keep the saints off their knees. When ever two saints met they invariably went to prayer. Today we can hardly be dragged to prayer." And, that was nearly one hundred years ago when Christians still prayed.

God give us prayer warriors!

"When a Christian shuns fellowship with other Christians, the devil smiles," says Corrie Ten Boom. "When he stops studying the Bible, the devil laughs. When he stops praying, the devil shouts for joy."

All too often, today, as soon as one knee hits the ground, the other is up and the prayer is over.

Pusillanimous pray-ers whisper tiptoe-through-the-tulip prayers. "God is great, God is good, let us thank Him for our food" and "Now I lay me down to sleep" prayers will not shake Heaven and move the earth. The church needs an Elijah.

Elijah prayed fervently. He cried out! There was power in His prayers. His prayers were effective. He prayed until the answer came.

Watchman Nee said, "Our prayers lay the track down on which God's power can come. Like a mighty locomotive, his power is irresistible, but it cannot reach us without rails." Who is laying the track in today's Pentecostal church?

The Master said, "My house shall be called the house of prayer" (Matthew 21:13). Yet, if the activities of any given church were divided into a pie chart, most often prayer would get the smallest piece of the pie. Thousands attend church worship services; hundreds attend church chicken dinners; dozens, or less, attend church prayer meetings.

Where are the Elijahs of the Lord God?

Elijah was also a man of great courage. He faced the king alone—a humble prophet challenging a powerful potentate. He was not afraid for his own life. He did not tell the king it would not rain for three years and six month. He told the king it would not rain again until he said so. Elijah was not worried about his reputation, God's reputation was on the line. When everyone else zigged, Elijah zagged!

Ahab, the wicked king, called Elijah the "troublemaker of Israel" (1Kings 18:17). He was not your run-of-the-mill, user-friendly, seeker-sensitive prophet. He was not molded by his culture. He was unafraid and unintimidated. God give us more "troublemakers."

As America's politicians and courts strip this nation of every vestige of its Christian heritage the church sits silent. May someone have the courage of Elijah and tell our spineless politicians that our school children *will* pray, we *will* celebrate the birth of our Lord and the Bible *will* remain the foundation of our great nation. Yes, that would cost something. True, biblical Christianity always does. Are we willing to pay the price? Does anyone have the courage?

This brave man also faced down the religious culture of the day. He confronted and killed the prophets of Baal, propagators of the most popular religion of the time.

Religion is the greatest enemy of revival. Only those brave enough to stand against the flow and defy the religious establishment will see God working in their lives and their generation.

Challenging the religious establishment is costly. It was the religious culture that nailed Jesus to His cross.

It was the religious culture that burned William Tyndale and John Huss on a stake.

It was the religious culture that threw Martin Luther out of the church.

It was the religious culture that banned John Wesley from the pulpits of the church he loved.

It was the religious culture that lambasted and buffooned William Seymour and the Azusa Street worshippers. The most vicious attacks came not from the secular press, but the conservative religious press.

Many men want to join the religious establishment and then improve it from within. Religion vehemently resists such renewal and reformers are seldom successful until the religious culture they hope to change spews them out. God told Elijah to draw a sword and kill it! The key to revival was not reformation but annihilation.

After courageously battling the political and religious culture, Elijah faced what was arguably the hardest task of all. He stood against Jezebel and the popular culture. There was one point where she almost got the best of him. Depressed and facing despair, the prophet wished to die, but God restored him and in the end he was triumphant.

Fifty years ago in America there was very little Christian television. Today some cable or satellite systems have a myriad of choices, twenty-four hours a day. There was little Christian radio fifty years ago. Many Christian radio ministers were charlatans broadcasting out of Mexico and trying to fleece their audience. Today, from one end of the radio dial to another there is wholesome Christian teaching and music. There were no mega churches fifty years ago. Now, we have many.

Yet, with all of this can anyone argue that America is a better nation today than fifty years ago? The culture is courser and the nation is less Christian. How could this be? At a time when the church seems to be advancing, society is going backwards.

Is the church ready to be honest? Can it handle the truth? Large congregations and bulging bank accounts are not the test of a healthy church.

The truth is, Christianity in America and through-out the western world is in decline—serious decline. Why? Instead of confronting the popular culture, the church has married it. Instead of influencing the world to become more Christian, the modern church has become more like the world.

The church has been dumbed down and dressed down. Church members and clergy alike have become pierced, stapled and inked to be like the world. The most awful and ungodly of the world's music has found its way into the house of the Lord. A church in Alabama uses the theme song from a sitcom about a bar as their meet and greet song. It doesn't seem to matter if the church mirrors the world, as long as it is a place "where everyone knows your name." Is there no limit to compromise?

America would see revival today if God could raise up an army of men like Elijah that were ready to plant their feet and stand—stand against the culture, the religious system and the political system.

There are other things we learn about Elijah. He was a man of deeds and not words. Elijah was no dreamer—he was a doer. When God said go, he didn't have to spend days deliberating over it or praying about it. When God said go, Elijah got up and went.

In the earliest days of Pentecost, missionaries would sense a call to a foreign land and within days or weeks they would be on their way. There were no committees, no boards, no hierarchy. They got their marching orders from heaven and march they did.

There is an old cliche—some people make things happen, some watch them happen and some just wonder what happened. Elijah made things happen. What kind of person are you?

Finally, Elijah was a man of faith.

It is great to be a man of courage.

It is great to be a man of action.

It is great to be a man of prayer.

None of this, alone, is enough. Any man or woman that wants to change their world must be a person of faith.

Elijah took God at His word. If God said it, Elijah believed it.

A popular Christian bumper sticker drapes the rear of many cars in the United States. Perhaps you have seen it, or even had one on your car. It says, "Jesus said it, I believe it, that settles it." Elijah always believed it and God settled it.

Saint Augustine said, "Faith is to believe what you do not see; the reward of this faith is to see what you believe." Amen.

When Elijah was on the mountain praying for rain, he continued to send his servant to look for a confirming sign. As soon as the servant reported a small cloud, Elijah was in motion. That was all he needed. He knew it was going to rain—God had said it would rain. Now, he knew when. Elijah believed God.

Jesus said, If thou canst believe, all things are possible to him that believeth" (Mark 9:23). Did He mean that? Of course He did. He is not a man that He could lie.

America can have revival. The church can be the church again. The violence in our streets can stop. The drug and alcohol culture can be defeated. Our course culture can be sanitized. Can you believe? Elijah did.

The Lord God of Elijah has not changed. He is as powerful today as He was two thousand or even two million years ago. His people have changed.

The church in America needs men and women who will swim against the current. Courageous men and women who will stand up to wickedness, wherever it raises its head—in the government, in the culture, in the church. America needs men and women who will pray, believe and work until change comes.

Where are the Elijahs of the Lord God ?

And the king of Israel said unto Jehoshaphat, There is yet one man, by whom we may enquire of the LORD: but I hate him, for he never prophesied good unto me, but always evil.

II Chronicles 18:7

THE PROPHET WHO NEVER SAID ANYTHING GOOD

Jehoshaphat was the king of Judah, a biblical monarchy made up of two tribes in the southern part of Israel. He was a godly man, but unfortunately, he was easily influenced by wicked colleagues as well.

Ahab, the king of Israel's ten northern tribes was a very evil despot. His wife, Jezebel, a Phoenician princess, was arguably the worst woman in the Bible. Together they formed a dastardly duo that allowed, or even advocated, idol worship among God's chosen. Their evil dynasty led the people away from righteousness and toward destruction.

The Syrians had been a constant threat to the northern kingdom. Although Ahab had driven the Syrian armies from most of his territories, they still held some of the northernmost cities, including the refuge city, Ramoth-Gilead. Ahab coveted a military coalition with Jehoshaphat so their combined armies could reclaim those cities.

More than three years earlier Ahab had led a successful war against the Syrians. Despite the wickedness of Ahab, God loved Israel and sent one of His true prophets who prophesied a great victory over this recurring enemy. With the help of God, Ahab had an opportunity to destroy the invading army and kill Benhadad, their wicked king. Instead, he entered into a covenant with Benhadad. God was very displeased with this unholy alliance, as He always is with such deals, and He sent a prophet to warn Israel's king, "Because thou hast let go out of thy hand a man whom I appointed to utter destruction, therefore thy life shall go for his life, and thy people for his people" (1 Kings 40:22).

As the present biblical account develops, Ahab is trying to seduce Jehoshaphat into an alliance. Ahab boasted, "My people are your people." This was true, but it was also so very false. Genetically and historically the people of the Israel and Judah were brothers. Spiritually, they were miles apart.

It is never the will of God for light to come into union with darkness. Jehosaphat was warned, "Shouldest thou help the ungodly, and love them that hate the Lord? (2 Chronicles 19:2). In the New Testament Paul expressed the mind of God in this same regard with his admonishment, "Be ye not unequally yoked together with unbelievers: for what fellowship hath righteousness with unrighteousness? and what communion hath light with darkness? (2 Corinthians 6:14).

Despite his weaknesses, Jehoshaphat had enough wisdom to seek God before joining Ahab in a war with the Syrians. He had heard from the iniquitous king of Israel, but he wanted to hear from God.

Ahab assembled four hundred of his best prophets. These were charter members of the king's "will-prophecy-for-food" brigade. Every man spoke with the same voice. "Go up," these prophets said, "God will deliver it into the king's hand."

Unifying around God's plan is always a good thing, but unanimity is no proof of God's will or purposes. Many in the church today are listening to one voice, but is it God's voice?

"The promotion of unity at the expense of truth is satanic; it is demonic; it is not true unity." said Daniel Webster, "It is not the unity of the Holy Spirit for He is the Spirit of Truth. The Scriptural command which we have in Ephesians to promote the unity of the Spirit and the bond of peace is given to those who have a common foundation of truth. Truth by its very nature divides. Where you have appeal to unity at the expense of truth all you have is uniformity."

Peruse a dozen Christian bookstores for the latest best-sellers on church success. Attend as many seminars on church planting, church growth and redevelopment. A handful of cathedrals of compromise have become the model for church success. It seems there is only one voice.

"Look at the size of their churches."

"Look at their success!"

The gurus of compromising Christianity speak with uniformity and unanimity. Gospel preaching has been replaced by pop psychology pep talks.

"Don't preach repentance."

"Don't preach the blood."

"Don't preach the cross."

"Don't offend."

Christian colleges and universities cut Christian ministers like cookies from the same broken mold.

"Go up," they say, "God will be with you." But is He? Is He really with them? Is church success measured only in bodies, budgets and buildings? Is God changing lives? Are these congregants any different from their colleagues in the world?

What if their faith demanded something? What if Christianity suddenly cost them? What if it cost them their lives? Of the thousands who attend church every Sunday how many would really give their all to Jesus?

Is this really the voice of God to the church? Is Christianity that costs nothing worth any more than it costs?

The truth is, God will allow a backslidden church to hear what it wants to hear! He will allow *you* to hear what you want to hear. If a Christless, crossless, costless gospel is what you are seeking, you can find it. There is no shortage of compromised churches.

God will allow you to believe what you want to believe—even to your own peril! You could stand on the deck of the Titanic and boast it isn't going to sink. You could say it until you perished in the chilly Atlantic.

To his credit, Jehoshaphat was not satisfied with Ahab's choir of prophets for hire. He asked, "is there not another prophet?" Jehoshaphat was looking for what a powerful preacher once called the "four-hundred-and-first prophet." Surely there was one prophet in Israel that had not sold out. Somewhere, there had to be a voice for the Lord.

Ahab said there is one more prophet, Micaiah, but I don't like him. He never says anything good about me. Micaiah didn't ride the popular bandwagon. He was unpopular and unwanted in his day. Would he fare any better today?

Should a pastor dare to say something bad he is quickly labeled as negative or judgmental. Nevermind the fact that what he says is true. Nevermind that it is the word of God. Christians today like good things said about them and there are plenty of false prophets willing to lie through their smile to tell bulging congregations that everything is good and God has a better life for everyone. Where are the Micaiahs? Where are the true prophets in the midst of this madness? Is there a word from the Lord?

Our ministry office frequently receives requests for prayer. The following was received recently and epitomizes the modern message, "I'm seeking prayer in my personal well being in success, joy, luck, money and love, happiness and good fortunes." Forget a message from God, "God give me luck, money and happiness. Amen."

Despite the reservations of Ahab, Micaiah was summoned.

What a charade ensued. One of the false prophets made horns of iron and put them on his head. He pranced around like a fool, announcing that in a similar manner Israel would push the Syrians back. The whole chorus chimed in. If these self-seeking seers had anything, they had harmony. They spoke with one voice, the voice of prosperity and victory. But, was it the voice of God?

The courier who fetched Micaiah for the king had a message for him. There was no need to cause any trouble. Four hundred prophets had all said the same thing. Everyone had said the king would be victorious in confronting the Syrians. The messenger had a recipe for popularity. All you have to do, he told Micaiah, is say the same thing everyone else is saying.

Micaiah was not for sale. "As the Lord liveth," he replied "what my God saith, that will I speak!" God give the Pentecostal church in America a modern day Micaiah! No, not one, but hundreds of faithful preachers that speak the truth like this priceless prophet.

Micaiah was brought to the gates of Samaria. Ahab and Jehosaphat were dressed in their royal robes and sitting on their respective thrones. Wealth, power and prestige looked down on a forlorn prophet. Intimidation was multiplied times two.

With the limited knowledge we have, it is hard to understand Micaiah's initial response. Like the false prophets he told the kings to go ahead and go up against the Syrians. Was the pressure too much for him? Did he cave to the imperial intimidation? Not likely. This prophet knew no fear. From the response of the kings, it seems he was merely toying with them. Micaiah was obviously facetious. What gave him away? Was it a cynical smile or a wry wink?

The king retorted, how many times do I have to adjure you, tell me nothing but the truth!

And, tell the truth is what Micaiah did.

The prophet said he saw the Jews as sheep that had no shepherd and a people with no master. With no one to lead them they should return to their homes in peace. Ahab was furious. Didn't I tell you he wouldn't say anything good about me, he complained.

Micaiah also saw a vision of God on His throne, surrounded by the angelic hosts. God was through with evil Ahab and was searching for a plan to dispose of him at Ramoth-Gilead. Several good ideas were proffered by the spirits around the throne, but one of God's servants suggested I can get him to Ramoth-Gilead by being a lying spirit in the mouth of his prophets.

Neither Ahab, nor his clueless prophets, knew they were merely pawns in God's plan, predicting their own demise. How many of today's parrot prophets are deceived by a lying spirit and are just as oblivious as these four-hundred fools.

Zedekiah slapped Micaiah on the face for telling the truth. Many of today's seeker sensitive shepherds don't have the wisdom to know that it is better to be smitten for righteousness than embraced by the unrighteous.

A slap is painful. Who wants to be struck in the face? Yet, Jesus said we are blessed when we are persecuted for the sake of right (Matthew 5:10). According to the Master, the "slapped" are the true heirs of the kingdom.

Ahab further ordered that Micaiah should be incarcerated, and afflicted with a diet of bread and water.

Hear this! Hear it and learn.

It is far better to be a true prophet, imprisoned and starving than to be a false prophet, free and feasting at Ahab's table.

Faced with prison and untold misery, Micaiah was still defiant. He told Ahab if he returned from Ramoth-Gilead then the Lord had not spoken. A true prophet doesn't get it right half the time or eighty percent of the time. God's prophet is right every time.

Stubborn and rebellious to the end, Ahab ignored the prophet's warning and went to battle against the Syrians. His intended goal, deliverance from this enemy, was a very good thing, but the end did not justify his evil and defiant means. Vance Havner said Ahab was a bad man doing a good thing in a wrong way.

Ahab tried several schemes to avoid his prophesied fate. He disguised himself in the uniform of a common soldier and even deflected attention from himself by insisting that Jehoshaphat wear his kingly robes. Was he foolish enough to think himself invincible? Did he think he could hide from the word of the Lord?

Mistaking Jehoshaphat for Ahab, the Syrian soldiers pursued him and would have killed him but for the grace of God. It appeared the wicked king had fooled the Syrians and cunningly thwarted the will of God as foretold my Micaiah. But, not quite. A Syrian soldier randomly shot an arrow toward the Israelite troops. Like David's stone, the arrow was divinely directed. It hit a chink in Ahab's armor and the wicked king perished on the battlefield. He was buried in Samaria and dogs drank his blood as had been foretold by Elijah, another of God's faithful prophets (1 Kings 21,22).

Ahab was a colorful, but tragic creature. Jehoshaphat, though a better man than his colleague, shifted like the wind. The only hero of this story is Micaiah, the uncompromising prophet.

America needs Micaiah today.

America needs a four-hundred-and-first prophet.

America needs a four-hundred-and-first church.

Unlike the current trend in Christianity, a four-hundred-and-first church is one where leaders are not led by manipulation and intimidation.

Look at the spiritual exploitation in this narrative. The lying prophet put iron horns on his head trying to influence the kings by his dramatic manipulation. It wasn't bad enough to be a false prophet—he was a bad actor, too.

Look at the intimidation Micaiah encountered. The courier that brought him to the king told him that everyone else was in agreement, speaking the same things. The easy road would have been to go along with the crowd.

Then, there was the pressure from authority—not just one king, but two. Shouldn't Micaiah have simply submitted to their authority and say what the kings wanted him to say and do what they wanted him to do? That is taught in many church circles today. Authoritarian leaders quote "touch not mine anointed" and demand unquestioned obedience. That is not leadership, that is manipulation.

The Bereans were more noble because they listened, questioned Paul's teachings and studied the scriptures for themselves. Church members need not accept false teaching. They need not allow accommodating shepherds to starve them on a watered-down gospel diet. A four-hundred-and-first church swims against the stream, refuses to walk in lock step with compromisers and resists the intimidation of the modern religious culture.

A four-hundred-and-first church hears from God. One church planter teaches that if a pastor wants to start a new church in a community he should go to Wal-mart and ask the people coming in and out what they think a good name for a church would be. A pioneering pastor should then launch his church based on this survey of unconverted people. Nonsense! The Western church resembles Oz's lion without courage, tin man with no heart and scarecrow with no brain.

Surely, we have lost our mind.

A true church and a true pastor don't get their marching orders from the latest best-seller at a Christian bookstore. They don't take a poll to see what is popular and they don't stick their finger in the air to see which way the wind is blowing. We need leaders like Micaiah who listen to the voice of God and speak only what He is speaking.

A four-hundred-and-first church tells the truth, the whole truth and nothing but the truth. There is great pressure today to change the gospel. The message of the cross is not accommodating enough. Many in the emergent church are teaching that everyone is saved. There are many ways to God, they boast. Blasphemy!

The truth is still the truth. Sin is still awful; Hell is still hot; and, Jesus is still the only way to Heaven. These eternal truths cannot and must not be compromised. To compromise is to lead men on a way that seems right, but the end is the way of death.

The ultimate goal might be to attract more people to the church and swell the rolls, but the end does not justify the perverted means. Are good men doing good things in a bad way? Does the kingdom of God profit when churches are filled with Christians with no commitment? Jesus told the hypocritical Pharisees that they would traverse the sea and land to make one proselyte and when they had recruited them, they were twice the children of hell as the Pharisees that converted them (Matthew 23:15). What of today's converts of convenience?"

Paul asked the Galatians, am I become your enemy because I tell you the truth? (Galatians 4:16). Who is the enemy of the church? The lying prophet or the one who never says anything good about the wicked, backslidden church?

A man bitten by a poisonous viper is looking for an antidote. If there is a cure, he wants it.

To this dying man with toxic venom in his veins, it matters not if the antidote is bitter.

It matters not how it tastes.

It matters not if it is hard to swallow.

Tell him you can water down the antidote to make it more pleasant, he will cry, "No give it to me straight."

Add sugar? No way.

He knows, the antidote is the only thing that can save him.

The gospel, the pure gospel—unadulterated, unabridged, and unchanged—is the only thing that saves today. The world doesn't need a pandering pastor peddling some palatable pablum. The world needs a prophet courageous enough to tell the truth without regard for how it tastes.

Finally, a four-hundred-and-first church has no agenda but God's.

The king's agenda is not their agenda.

The culture's agenda is not their agenda.

The Pope's agenda is not their agenda.

The denomination's agenda is not their agenda. They are following God!

Today, the primary goal of many churches is to grow bigger campuses, bigger congregations and bigger coffers. This is man's agenda, not God's.

No, it is not wrong to have a growing church. Healthy churches will grow. It is a very good thing. The church in Acts is an excellent example of a growing church—spreading from their own communities to all the known world.

But, numerical and physical growth must be secondary to spiritual growth. God's agenda is spiritual maturity and self-sacrifice. God's agenda always involves an altar. Despite the name over the door, a building filled with non-converted, non-committed and non-consecrated "Christians" is not a church.

God's agenda is expensive. It cost Micaiah his freedom. It cost Jesus His life. It will cost you something. What did it cost you this week?

Enter ye in at the strait gate: for wide is the gate, and broad is the way, that leadeth to destruction, and many there be which go in thereat: Because strait is the gate, and narrow is the way, which leadeth unto life, and few there be that find it.

Matthew 7:13-14

THE NARROW WAY

The Christian church is under attack today as never before. The popular culture hates the church. One television show after another buffoons and besieges the Christian faith. If a token believer is added to the cast of characters, they are portrayed as either judgmental, dishonest or inept.

At the same time, homosexuals are almost always featured in a positive light. Judging by the number of homosexuals on television sitcoms, one could guess that gays and lesbians are a majority of the population, rather than the reality of less than four percent.

The entertainment culture is getting courser by the year. "Wardrobe malfunctions" have given way to outright obscenity. For decades, Hollywood has been at war with Christian morality. Sorry to say, Hollywood is winning. Cable programs opened the floodgates and now the American airways are drowning in smut and anti-God brainwashing.

The political culture hates the church. The United States was clearly founded by Christian men, establishing a government based on Christian principles. Throughout our history our presidents, legislators and justices have declared this is a "Christian nation."

One would hardly know that today. Courts and laws are openly hostile to the Christian faith. President Barack Obama declared to the world we Americans "do not consider ourselves a Christian nation." Perhaps he is right. I hope not! The secularist in government have done everything in their power to strip this great nation of every vestige of our Christian heritage.

The liberal educational culture hates the church. Everyone is grateful for teachers. They work hard and are often underpaid and under-appreciated. At the same time public education unions are blatantly anti-Christian. Classrooms are pummeled with pro-homosexual, pro-Moslem and anti-American propaganda. The religion of the American classroom is secular humanism and unions and administrators make sure the entire educational system worships at the humanistic altar. Faith in God, once the foundation of our educational system, has been replaced by faith in science and psychology.

Christmas celebrations are not allowed in public schools. Christian holiday greetings are forbidden, Christmas trees and in some cases even Santa Clauses are outlawed. In the same classrooms the occultic facets of a once Christian "All Hallowed Eve'n" are celebrated with all the demons, witches and ghosts the schools can conjure.

While Christianity is the kryptonite of public schools, tolerance of other religions, especially Islam is promoted. One public school in Colorado recently forced chorale members to sing a Muslim song with lyrics which included "There is no truth except Allah" and "Allah is the only eternal and immortal." One can only imagine the uproar if the name "Jesus" was substituted for "Allah."

The same schools that require gay-centric curriculum, explicit sex education and Darwinistic evolution for elementary students, expel Christian students for wearing shirts with a Christian witness. Tolerance is little less than a god in public schools but there is no tolerance of God.

Elementary students have been embarrassed when the saying of grace at the lunch table has led to a trip to an administrator's office. High school seniors whose scholarship earned them the privilege of speaking to their peers through a salutatory or valedictory speech have been forbidden to pray or even mention the name of Jesus.

What could illustrate the anti-Christian bias and politically correct nonsense more than the public schools in New Haven, Connecticut, who have removed "in the year of our Lord" from high school diplomas? Institutional education has declared war on the Christian faith.

The popular culture hates the church.

The political culture hates the church.

The educational culture hates the church.

So what? Does it really matter? Hell has always hated the church.

Thank God, Jesus said that not even the gates of hell could prevail against the church (Matthew 16:18). Secular humanism, political correctness and gay rights will not prevail against the church. The church has often prospered in seasons of persecution. But, the greatest threat to the church comes from none of these. The greatest threat to the church is from the religious culture. Religion doesn't hate the church like so much of modern culture. It is supported by too many of its various enterprises. It just hates the godly goals of a true New Testament church.

Religion wants to destroy the church from within. The Greeks couldn't conquer ancient Troy from without so they devised a plan to get inside the fortified city. A Trojan horse opened the door for a Greek victory. Compromise is the Trojan horse of the Christian church.

Religion doesn't want to end Christianity, it wants to render it useless by changing it, diluting it. Religion wants to broaden the way.

Jesus says the way is narrow.

Modern churches say come and join us, we will make it easy for you. It will cost you nothing. We will even give you cappuccinos, donuts and jungle gyms for your kids just to entice you to come. These amenities may not be wrong, but this is a million miles from New Testament Christianity when the severe judgement of God frightened the unrepentant away (Acts 5:5).

An Assemblies of God church in Missouri recently opened an extension campus in a former bar. The local newspaper reported the church "looked like a nightclub ready to rock." The reporter was kind in saying the style of the church was "slightly irreverent." Sermons in the church include "Bible Girls Gone Wild" and "Whoopee Cushion Life."

One attendee said worshipping at the church was more like her secular life than her previous church life. The most descriptive—and also most damning—quote came from a lady who said, *"You don't have to change to be here."* Is this a narrow way?

Not long ago, every Assemblies of God minister in America would drop their head in shame at such antics. Now, many stand and applaud. Because the building is full, many denominational leaders see this as a model church for the twenty-first century. This type of church is called "cutting edge." Perhaps, "Trojan Horse" would better characterize the church's approach.

Is this really Christianity? Does it in any way resemble the church of the New Testament? James, the brother of Jesus wrote, "whosoever therefore will be a friend of the world is the enemy of God" (James 4:4). Is the modern Western church God's enemy?

The narrow way is paved with convictions. There was a time when Pentecostal believers had personal convictions that effected every area of their life. They dressed differently. They avoided secular sports and entertainments. Perhaps these things were not a sin.

Perhaps they weren't clearly prohibited in the Bible, but they didn't do these things because God had spoken to them and they had convictions. They knew that not everything that hindered in the Christian race was a sin, some things were merely weights (Hebrews 12:1). But they wanted nothing to slow them down.

The narrow way leaves little room for self. In fact, Jesus said to follow Him a man or woman would have to deny themselves and take up a cross (Matthew 16:24). Has the church forgotten that Jesus said that? Does it care?

He went further to say if anyone didn't take up the cross, they were not worthy of Him (Matthew 10:38). When He said take a cross, He didn't mean to wear a gold cross and chain or put a fish decal on your bumper. When He says take your cross, He is talking about death.

"What is lacking today is not a better living but a better dying," said China's most famous preacher, Watchman Nee.

Death to sin.

Death to self.

Death to the easy way.

Taking up a cross costs something.

"If I see aright, the cross of popular evangelicalism is not the cross of the New Testament," wrote Tozier. "It is, rather, a new bright ornament upon the bosom of a self-assured and carnal Christianity. The old cross slew men, the new cross entertains them. The old cross condemned; the new cross amuses. The old cross destroyed confidence in the flesh; the new cross encourages it."

What cross do you carry?

Carrying a biblical cross and walking the narrow way requires a strict adherence to biblical standards. Satan's trick in the garden was to get Eve to doubt the truth of God's word. The word of God is in Satan's cross hairs again today. The church does not have to deny the Bible to lose its effectiveness, it merely has to doubt it.

While attending a Pentecostal seminary I saw first hand how that religion wants to broaden the way. I was told the Bible was the word of God and the *truths* it contained were infallible—not the Bible, mind you, just the truths it contained. I was told that we couldn't really know that the gospels contained the actual words of Jesus. The narrative, they said, evolved with the growing church.

On and on it goes . . .

"The serpent that bit Paul wasn't really deadly. There were no poisonous snakes on that island."

"It took a long time to make the Grand Canyon."

"God didn't really strike Ananias and Sapphira dead. It was coincidental that they died at that time."

When the church no longer believes the Bible is true, the way can get really broad. Living in adultery isn't so bad any more. Homosexuality isn't really a sin. Don't you know they were born that way? The Assemblies of God recently changed its position on ordaining homosexuals from a "no way, no how, not now, not ever" policy to leniency on those who are not "practicing" the sin. Have they caved to the societal lie? Is it permissible to have homosexual desires as long as you are celibate? What is the perversion? The practice of sodomy or the very heart of the sodomite? How could a loving God condemn gays, lesbians and the transgendered to hell if He made them the way they are?

The church is told to ignore particular passages that condemn sin and focus on the overall themes of the Bible, like love and forgiveness. The Bible is so watered down in many churches it has lost its power. Even the way to heaven is broader in today's church. Popular preachers can't go on television and unequivocally declare that Jesus in the only way to God. Preachers who speak in tongues and claim to love God and His word say that everyone will ultimately be saved. Can the way become any broader than that?

Intimidated by popular culture, Christians are afraid to be called narrow minded or offensive. These words are the scarlet letters of today's church.

Jesus was very narrow minded. He said there was only one way to heaven and it was a narrow way. He said, "I am the way." There is no way but Him. That is very narrow.

Jesus constantly offended people. He offended them on purpose. He said the religious leaders of His day were snakes and hypocrites. He wasn't obnoxious, but He was offensive. Offending sinful desires is no crime and demands no apology.

Jesus said the way to heaven was narrow and few would find it. This stands in stark contrast to a Christian church that opens their membership to everyone without conversion or commitment to Christ.

Many in the emerging church believe Muslims will be in heaven.

Buddhist will be in heaven.

Hindus will be in heaven.

Atheists will be in heaven

Backslidden Christians will be in heaven.

To hear some tell it everyone will be there. When a popular entertainer dies after a career of abusing drugs and alcohol, they are eulogized as near-saints. Christian pastors and prophets promote them right into paradise. Has God closed hell? Does He no longer need it? According to the broad way, the righteous and unrighteous are all going to Heaven. Today, in many churches the way is so broad that many of their members are no longer on the real road. Without knowing it they have strayed and are off on the shoulder somewhere or even in a ditch. Sadder still, the American church has led them to believe that everything is fine and they are still on the road. Or, worst of all, that the ditch is as good as the road.

Jesus said otherwise, He said the way is narrow and "few" would find it.

Are you one of the few?

Have you found it? What did it cost you?

*The sluggard will not plow by reason of the cold;
therefore shall he beg in harvest, and have nothing.*

Proverbs 20:4

HOW DID WE GET HERE?

Years ago the great Baptist pastor Jack Hyles preached a sermon on compromise. Perhaps all of his sermons touched on compromise. In this message Hyles, no friend of Pentecostals, was lamenting the decline of the Assemblies of God. He said something like this, "Assembly of God people don't live for God. There was a time when their women didn't wear makeup and now their men do."

Burt Clendennen an icon of the Assemblies of God once said, "When I got into this movement you couldn't wear a watch now we have people who don't wear anything."

"My dear old mother wore more clothes to bed . . . than women wear to church these days," said Evangelist Don Brankel.

Of course, these men were speaking in hyperbole—or were they? There has certainly been drastic changes in the Pentecostal movement. Until at least the 1950s most Pentecostal people were called "holiness" because of their conservative life-styles. How many would use that term to describe Pentecostals today?

Not too long ago, Pentecostal churches railed on the public schools for promoting dancing. In some cases they were successful in cancelling school proms for decades. Now, they clear the chairs from their sanctuaries and host dances with their youth gyrating to rock bands. Pentecostal preachers once condemned secular music and now it is becoming a part of Sunday morning services.

Recently a youth teacher's Sunday School lesson had a note indicating that social drinking was acceptable. Is that hyperbole? Radiant Life quickly apologized and affirmed the Assemblies of God position on abstinence from alcohol, but that begs the bigger question—how did those comments get into Assemblies of God Sunday school materials? Who wrote the lesson? Who edited it? With all the talent in the movement, has the training of Pentecostal youth been contracted out to writers who don't share our standards?

In other countries the change is even more shocking. In Australia, under the leadership of Hillsong churches, the Assemblies of God have changed their name to Australian Christian Churches. While their code of conduct for ministers once recommended that ministers should abstain from alcohol, now it suggests they shouldn't get drunk. A former pastor with the group told me that after a recent denominational meeting they chartered a bus and took their ministers to a nightclub.

One visitor described the Sunday Hillsong service as "a Justin Beiber type pop show with nauseating 'Jesus is my boyfriend' Jesus Jingles repeated ad nauseam." With strobe lights and fog machines the church services look far more like a rock concert than a worship venue.

Along with the Assemblies of God tag, Hillsong has also abandoned many of their Pentecostal roots. Repentance is down played. One speaker at a recent conference said repentance was about "relational restoration" and not "behavioral modification." Someone should inform John the Baptist.

This is the same group that chose "This Is Revival" for their annual slogan.

Are they serious?

Have we lost our minds?

Early Pentecostals were distinctive in their dress. Pentecostal women often wore white and were very simple in there accessories. Today Pentecostal women are often as immodest as their ungodly neighbors. Men, even pastors, are stapled, pierced, punctured and tattooed. One Assemblies of God pastor took all of his staff to get a tattoo as if it were some rite of passage. A musician on the platform of a Pentecostal church wore a belt emblazoned with "I Love Boobies" in bold letters.

Is this nonsense born of a desire to be more like Jesus? or a desire to be more like the world? The question is rhetorical and the answer is obvious.

In the entire history of the Christian church there has probably not been a single revival movement that has changed so much in such a short time.

Not all the changes have been in life-style. There have been significant changes in doctrine and liturgy.

Although most of the mainline Pentecostal churches still hold to the same doctrines in theory, in practice things have changed dramatically. Churches have de-emphasized the rapture theology and most other eschatology. Many Pentecostals no longer hold speaking in tongues to be the initial physical evidence of the Holy Spirit baptism. In some Pentecostal churches less than half of the congregants speak in tongues. In some cases, much less. Are these still "Pentecostal" churches?

Recently, while sitting in a Sunday school class in an Assembly of God church I was surprised to hear the teacher say, "Sins committed tomorrow are already forgiven today." No one in the class seemed to disagree, I'm not even sure they cared. Can we lean any further toward Calvinism without falling completely in?

Divine healing was once a mainstay in Pentecostal circles, now many churches never anoint with oil and offer prayer for the sick. Those who do offer prayers often retreat to praying for wisdom and skills for the medical team, rather than miracles, signs and wonders.

Worship that was once so emotional and boisterous that it was called "Holy Roller" has been largely replaced by stoic services that more closely resemble a Presbyterian church than a Pentecostal church of seventy-five years ago or else a bump and grind, smoke and light, rock and roll show. Messages in tongues were once so common in Pentecostal churches that they had to be regulated. Today they are almost nonexistent. When such manifestations do happen they are relegated to some back room so guests won't be offended by a move of the Holy Spirit. To borrow a phrase, "You've come a long way, baby."

Only those who never experienced real Pentecost could label all of this as progress. While advancing in numbers, the Pentecostal movement has lost serious spiritual ground.

How has this happened? How did we get here?

As strange as it may seem, the answer may well be found in Proverbs 20:4. If a person is too lazy to prepare the soil when the time is right, the writer says, then they will have nothing to eat at harvest time.

But, what does this have to do with the church today? Nineteenth century cleric, Alexander

MacLaren found three powerful truths in this text: 1) present conduct determines future conditions, 2) the easy road is usually the wrong one, 3) the season let slip is gone forever. These principles hold the secret to what has gone so badly wrong in the Pentecostal movement and the Western church as a whole.

First, consider this, present conduct determines future conditions. Picture a great marathon runner as he crosses the finish line. Twenty-six miles of grueling race is behind him. His joy at being the first to break the ribbon is indescribable. This athlete did not start preparing for the competition yesterday. It takes more than willpower to win the race. It takes extensive preparation and training—sometimes years of training. The runner's conduct yesterday is what wins the race today.

How about the man climbing Mount Everest, the earth's tallest mountain? Do you think he got there in a day? Most likely he spent years preparing financially, physically and mentally for the climb. The climber's past conduct determines his success or failure.

In Galatians 6:7 Paul wrote, "Be not deceived; God is not mocked: for whatsoever a man soweth, that shall he also reap." What a person or movement does today determines their future.

For good or bad, your today is the result of your yesterday and your tomorrow will be the result of your today.

Early Pentecostal pioneers walked the streets with Bible in hand. They preached, they witnessed, they sacrificed. Unafraid and unembarrassed they stood on street corners and sang and preached and prayed. Wherever they traveled they put up tents and brush arbors and proclaimed the good news. Everything they did was baptized in tears.

They preached it straight—sin was ugly and hell was hot. But, they lived what they preached. They often lived on little or nothing, but they trusted God and not man for their provision. "Benefit packages" were not part of their vocabulary.

Every Pentecostal church was revivalistic in its approach. Many congregations would hold services every night of the week. Guest evangelists would stay for weeks and months as the Lord of the Harvest gathered golden sheaves.

Because of their self-sacrifice the Pentecostal movement saw years of unparalleled growth. What they did in the teens, twenties and thirties brought a great harvest even into the sixties and seventies. Past performance brought present results.

Then they stopped. Maybe it isn't possible to mark a date or time, but they stopped. They stopped prayer meetings; they stopped street meetings; they stopped revival meetings. Now, a significant number of the major Pentecostal denominations in the western word have entered a season of stagnation. Most, if they are growing at all, are only growing in the addition of ethnic congregations where the modern religious culture of compromise has had less influence.

The future for the Pentecostal movement in the west, except for a major revival, will be even worse.

What the church is sowing today it will reap tomorrow. If Christianity costs nothing today it will be worth nothing tomorrow. God help us.

American culture is polluted today because of what the church tolerated yesterday. What will tomorrow look like?

Compromise today will cripple the church tomorrow.

Someone, somewhere, please put a trumpet to your lips. Sound the alarm. It is revival or die.

Secondly, MacLaren said, the easy road is usually the wrong one. How profound is that?

Today, we say if it sounds too good to be true, it probably is. Hear this, if a Christianity that costs nothing sounds too good to be true—it is because it is too good to be true! It is a lie. True biblical Christianity costs everything.

America's most famous colonial pastor, Jonathan Edwards, said "The way to heaven is ascending, we must be content to travel uphill, though it be hard and tiresome, and contrary to the natural bias of the flesh."

The story is told of a university that devised a test by placing ten students in a room. The professor had a card with three lines on it, each line a different length. Students were to raise their hands when the instructor pointed to the longest line. Nine of the ten students were told in advance to raise their hand, not for the longest line, but the second longest. The tenth student was the patsy. In three out of four instances the dupe would raise their hand and then bring it back down when they realized they were the only one with a raised hand.

It was easier to be comfortable than right. But the easy road was the wrong road. It takes courage to swim upstream. Standing against the religious culture, the political culture and the entertainment culture is a frightening prospect. Admiral Eddie Rickenbacker said, "Courage is doing what you're afraid to do. There can be no courage unless you're scared." It is easier to go with the flow, but the flow is going in the wrong direction. The church needs courageous men and women who will arise like an army and choose the narrow way.

The people's poet, Edward A. Guest penned these prophetic words:

> The easy roads are crowded
> And the level roads are jammed;
> The pleasant little rivers
> With the drifting folk are crammed.
> But off yonder where it's rocky,
> Where you get a better view,
> You will find the ranks are thinning
> And the travelers are few.
>
> Where the going's smooth and pleasant
> You will always find the throng,
> For the man, more's the pity,
> Seem to like to drift along.
> But the steeps that call for courage,
> And the task that's hard to do,
> In the end result in glory
> For the never-wavering few.

On December 1, 1955, seamstress Rosa Parks refused to give up her seat on a Montgomery, Alabama bus. The driver insisted that she move in deference to a white passenger, but Rosa said no. It would have been simpler to have just moved. Rosa lost her job because she wouldn't move. Giving up her seat would have been the easy road, but it would have been the wrong road.

Rosa's actions started a bus boycott in Montgomery. The strike put Martin Luther King in the national spotlight. She is called "the mother of freedom." The difficult road was the right road. America is a better country because of Rosa Parks. To honor her courageous stand for civil rights, Rosa received the Presidential Medal of Freedom and the Congressional Gold Medal. At her death, she was the first woman to lie in state at the United States Capitol.

Believers who choose the right road will receive a much greater reward. They will be honored in heaven. Those who choose the easy road will receive nothing.

Some today would blame all the woes of the Pentecostal movement on a few prominent personalities that experienced failures in the 1980s. That is silly nonsense. A very wise man said, "For a just man falleth seven times, and riseth up again" (Proverbs 24:16). To blame the dilemma in Pentecostalism on a single man would be as foolish as blaming all of Israel's backsliding on David's shortcomings. The church is not in trouble because a few fell, the church is in trouble because many will not stand.

Noah took the hard road. It is difficult to imagine the immensity of his task—building that huge boat and then loading so many animals. He must have borne the scorn and ridicule of a thousand neighbors. But then the flood came and Noah was saved. The easy road would have meant death for the prophet and his family.

Daniel could have taken the easy road. He could have succumbed to pressure and compromised a little. He could have closed his windows and prayed in secret. Because he prayed openly, defying the king's edict, he was thrown into a den of lions. But, in answer to his courage he learned about divine deliverance. The easy road would have been the wrong road.

The three Hebrews could have bowed before the king's idol. Surely it would have been acceptable to bow just a little. Who would have known? They were hundreds of miles from home. They could have compromised.

David didn't have to face Goliath. Everyone else, including King Saul and his own three brothers, were cowering before the taunts of the giant. David could have taken the easy road back to his father. His siblings would have celebrated his departure. Instead, he asked who is this uncircumcised Philistine to defy the armies of God. David went against the grain.

Paul could have chosen an easier path. There was a huge price tag on his walk with Christ. He was shipwrecked, whipped, beaten, stoned and finally beheaded for his faith. It cost him a great deal to be a Christian, but because of his sacrifice, the church has benefited for two thousand years. Any other road for Paul would have been the wrong road.

Simon Peter, facing death, was crucified upside down at his own request. He didn't feel worthy to die as Jesus did. Christianity cost him something. He could have chosen an easier road.

Look at the road Jesus took. He didn't have to leave heaven. He didn't have to come to the earth and die. He chose the way of sacrifice for the salvation of humankind. It seems an understatement to say he did not choose the easy road. Now, without apology, He asks men to take the narrow road for Him. It is the only reasonable response.

Vance Havner said, "Jesus Christ demands more complete allegiance than any dictator who ever lived. The difference is, He has a right to it." His way is a narrow way.

Any other road is the wrong road. The church in America is in decline because it has chosen the easier road.

If a wise man loses his way, he will go back to the place he made a wrong turn and get back on the right road. Pentecostal leaders must know we are on the wrong road. Even the statistics prove it. Why don't they point their congregations back to the narrow way that once worked so well for the church? Instead they flay around looking for a hundred other easy roads?

Finally, consider MacLaren's third point, the season let slip is gone forever. Revivalist Leonard

Ravenhill said it like this, "The opportunity of a lifetime must be seized within the lifetime of the opportunity."

In 2 Corinthians 6:2, the great apostle reminds us "behold, now is the accepted time; behold, now is the day of salvation." We graciously describe God as the God of the second chance, but many have had only one chance. Some have had none.

In the early days of sailing, a ship could not enter the port until the high tide. The Latin expression for this is *ob portu*. The ship is waiting off the port until the moment that the rising tide will allow entrance into the harbor. From the Latin term we get our English word "opportunity." The ship's crew would wait patiently for that one opportunity to reach the harbor. If they were not diligent and missed the moment, they would have to wait for the next tide to roll in.

What could be sadder than missing God's opportunity? There may be only one chance. Every sign points to the fact that Jesus is coming soon. The world cannot continue on its current path to holocaust. He could come today and the church's chance to make a difference in the world would end. The tide will not rise again.

Even if Christ should tarry His coming, how long will a backsliding church continue to have any influence on society? Some studies say as many as two-third of Christian youth are leaving the church. Perhaps the easy road isn't working as well for us as has been suggested.

More than a century ago, Charles Spurgeon, the prince of preachers, believed "that one reason why the church of God at this present moment has so little influence over the world is because the world has so much influence over the church." What would he say now? Will the worldly church of today have *any* influence tomorrow?

This is the accepted time. At the great Brownsville Revival, night after night Evangelist Steve Hill reminded the audience, "Tomorrow is a word found only in a fool's dictionary."

This is our day of salvation.

Popular legend says that Nero fiddled while Rome burned. What is the church doing while western culture is going to hell in a hand basket? Is the church fiddling?

God will judge every generation according to the opportunities He has given. In Luke 12:48, Jesus said, "For unto whomsoever much is given, of him shall be much required." Can anyone say that America and all the western world has not been given much?

Jesus pronounced a special woe on the cities of Chorazin and Bethsaida, saying Tyre and Sidon would have repented if they had had the same opportunities as these two wicked cites. The greater the opportunity missed, the greater the judgement. Would Tyre and Sidon have repented if they had the same opportunities America has had? What will the "woe" be for this country if we miss our chance?

The conservative Methodist evangelist Sam P. Jones said there were three kinds of people—opportunity makers, opportunity takers and opportunity breakers. The woman at the well saw an opening and took it. She was an opportunity taker. Nicodemus went searching for Jesus by night. He was an opportunity maker. The rich young ruler had salvation handed to him but he left lost and defeated. He was an opportunity breaker.

What is the church in America?

An opportunity taker?

An opportunity maker?

An opportunity breaker? What are you?

Never in the history of the Christian church has the opportunity been so great. The western church has the resources and the technologies to reach the world for Christ. The church has the capacity to change the ever coarsening culture. It has done neither. Will it now rise to the occasion? Or will the church be an opportunity breaker and continue to compromise its way into irrelevance?

One of the saddest texts in the Bible is Jeremiah 8:20. The weeping prophet wistfully writes, "The harvest is past, the summer is ended, and we are not saved."

The harvest is passing. The summer is ending.

Will the world be saved?

Will you be saved?

Shadrach, Meshach, and Abednego, answered and said to the king, O Nebuchadnezzar, we are not careful to answer thee in this matter. If it be so, our God whom we serve is able to deliver us from the burning fiery furnace, and he will deliver us out of thine hand, O king. But if not, be it known unto thee, O king, that we will not serve thy gods, nor worship the golden image which thou hast set up.

Daniel 3:16-18

THE FIFTH LEVEL OF FAITH

For years, Israel was in a cycle of backsliding, repentance and revival. The unfaithfulness of the Jews weighed on the patience of a very longsuffering God.

Politically, the Jewish state had been partially under the control of the Assyrian empire for decades. The Syrians were defeated by the Babylonians late in the seventh century BC. The Egyptians fearing the power of Babylon moved preemptively to possess Israel and much of Syria. The Babylonians launched a counter offensive and during the ensuing battles Josiah the king of Judah was killed and Israel became a client state of the Babylonian empire.

In 606 BC, Nebuchadnezzar chose several gifted young Jews of royal descent to study in Babylon. They were to learn the language, literature and customs of Babylon and serve in the king's court. Among the captives were Daniel, Hananiah, Mishael, and Azariah. As part of their assimilation into Babylonian culture, each was given a new pagan name, Belteshazzar, Shadrach, Meshach, and Abednego, respectively.

The first test for the Hebrews came when they were ordered to partake of meat and wine from the king's table. More than likely the cuisine had been defiled by first being offered to false gods. There was also the strong possibility that the menu contained meats forbidden in the law God had given to Moses. Remaining faithful to the law of God, the Hebrews asked to be excused from the delicacies of Nebuchadnezzar's kitchen. Their request could have been interpreted as an insult to the culture and could have cost them their lives. Doing right is often costly.

The Hebrews were given a ten day reprieve during which time they would only eat vegetables and drink water. God was with them and after ten days on their kosher diet, they appeared healthier than their comrades who ate the king's finer foods. This must have been a great faith builder for these young men held prisoner in a foreign land.

A greater challenge came when the ego-driven Nebuchadnezzar raised a statue of himself in the Plain of Dura. The figure was made of gold and some say it stood nine-stories high. He ordered that everyone in the surrounding area would bow before the image and demonstrate their allegiance to his dominion. To fail to bow would bring a terrible death in a fiery furnace.

Someone in the crowd noticed that Shadrach, Meshach, and Abednego did not bow. They could not bow. To do so would have been a denial of their Jewish faith. God's law doesn't bow to man's law.

The three were brought before the king who gave them a second chance to follow the edict. Their answer was uncompromising. They said, "Our God whom we serve is able to deliver us from the burning fiery furnace, and He will deliver us out of your hand, O king. But if He doesn't, know this O king, that we will not serve your gods, nor worship the golden image which you have set up."

When carefully dissected, five levels of faith in God can be found in their answer. First they said "Our God." This is foundational. The writer of Hebrews said to have faith one must first believe that God is (Hebrews 11:6).

This is more than a tacit admission that there is a God, this is to believe that He is who He says He is. He is the creator of all the universe. Genesis 1:1, the first verse of the Bible, says that in the beginning God created the heavens and the earth. If a person has faith to believe that, they can believe everything else in the Bible. Isn't it convenient, the first verse in the book is the hardest one to believe. Take God at His word on Genesis 1:1 and the rest is easy.

There is no problem believing the sun went backwards or that a donkey talked, if you can believe that God made everything that is out of nothing that was. On the other hand, anyone who cannot accept, by simple faith, that God is the Creator will struggle with everything else in the Bible.

The Psalmist wrote, "The fool has said in his heart, There is no God" (Psalm 14:1). In case anyone missed it he said it again in Psalm 53: 1. There is, however, a greater fool. This is the person who knows there is a God but does not serve Him.

The Hebrews were no fools. The second phrase in their response is "whom we serve." They not only believed in God, they served Him. They had already proven that when they refused the king's meat and wine.

Paul said, "I know whom I have believed" (2 Timothy 1:12). Paul believed in God. He believed enough to serve Him. There is no other explanation for why he crisscrossed the known world, working under indescribable duress.

This is why he submitted to the humiliation, to the deprivation, to the pain. This is why he went to Jerusalem knowing through the prophets that he would be imprisoned. This is why he went to Rome and gave his life in martyrdom.

He believed in God and he served Him. He gave everything he had.

What does this say about the cost-cutting Christianity offered in so many American churches? What a person believes affects their manner of living. How can someone claim they believe in God and His son Jesus and not serve Him?

Do you believe in God? Do you believe Him enough to serve Him? Really? Does it affect the way you live? What did it cost you this week?

Salvation is free, it is the gift of God through His son, Jesus. Discipleship, on the other hand, costs everything. Are we not called to be His disciples?

Next, in their answer to Nebuchadnezzar the Hebrews said these two words "will deliver." They believed God had the power to deliver His people from trouble.

This is actually the second foundation of faith. The first was the belief in God and the second is to believe "He is a rewarder of them that diligently seek Him" (Hebrews 11:16).

God is not some distant someone who never interferes in the affairs of men. The Deists believe that God is real; that perhaps He was the creator; but, He is not involved in the daily operation of the universe He created. They compare God to a clock maker. He makes the clock, winds it and then leaves it to run on its own.

That is not the God of the Bible. The God of the Bible cares about you. He cares about your problems. He is able to deliver you.

The examples are too numerous to mention. When the children of Israel were in the bondage of Egypt, God cared enough to deliver them. When they came to the Red Sea, with Pharaoh's army in hot pursuit, He parted the waters for them to cross over on a dry seabed. For forty years He fed them and clothed them in the wilderness. When they came to Jericho, He miraculously brought the walls down. It seems He is very involved in His creation.

God is still concerned about the needs of His children. The Bible was written thousands of years ago, but God has not changed. He is still the "rewarder" of those that seek Him. The late R. W. Shambach must have said it ten thousand times, "You don't have any trouble! All you need is faith in God." Amen.

Now it gets personal. They said, He is able to deliver "us." This is a higher level of faith. It is not too hard for Pentecostals to believe that God delivered people in the Bible. Most take God at His word. Sometimes it is even easier to believe that God will deliver someone else. That is distant, theoretical, faith in the abstract.

The Hebrews didn't just believe God was able to deliver, they believed He was able to deliver them. Their faith was specific and explicit, not generic or vague.

Peter told believers to cast "all your care upon him; for he careth for you" (1 Peter 5:7). God is not just concerned about the needs of others, He cares for you! He is your deliverer.

For most, this is the highest level of faith. Receiving from God to most "faith teachers" is the ultimate. Many people never get to this fourth dimension of faith, and those who do seldom get any further. But there is something better than being faith filled, it is to be *faithful*.

Shadrach, Meshach and Abednego had a higher level of faith. It is the fifth level and is found in these three words, "but if not." Some would argue this was doubt, perhaps even unbelief. Not so. This is faith at its best. This is faithfulness.

They knew God could and would deliver them, but if for any reason He did not, they were going to remain faithful. If it cost them their lives to serve God, so be it.

Too many people look at God like Santa Clause. If they don't get what they want from His sack of goodies they get angry. Some even backslide over a prayer that wasn't answered to their satisfaction. This is childish, immature, insane.

Real faith realizes it may cost something to be a Christian. It may cost everything. If it does, real faith still serves Him.

This is the kind of faith Jesus had. Once again, this defines the *kenosis* of Christ. He didn't have to come to earth and die. He could have been saved by a legion of angels. He knew, better than any of us know, that God could deliver Him from this agony. But God didn't. Death, not deliverance was God's plan. Christ was faithful. The deliverance came later. Can you be faithful when deliverance doesn't come on your schedule? Can you serve Him when it costs you something?

Job said, "Though he slay me, yet will I trust in him" (Job 13:15). He then said, after I have been tried "I shall come forth as gold" (Job 23:10). Deliverance came for Job, but it wasn't cheap. It cost him first. Through his trials, Job was faithful.

As Abraham and his son climbed the mount of sacrifice, he knew that God would provide. He even testified to it. Still, he was willing to kill Isaac on the altar if that is what God required of him. He had faith, but more important, he was faithful. He was righteous.

When Peter and John were arrested and incarcerated for preaching the gospel, freedom was easily within their reach. All they had to do was take the easy road. Just stop preaching Jesus. Realizing how much it could cost them, they replied, "we cannot but speak the things which we have seen and heard" (Acts 4:20). Deliverance is great. Obedience is better. Later, it cost Peter his life. His was the greatest example of faith.

Compromise could have saved John Huss from the stake. Death was better than deliverance. John Bunyan could have been "delivered" from Bedford prison on many occasions. He stood for right. It cost him dearly. He was faithful.

Missionary Jim Elliot and his four comrades did not have to die in the jungles of Ecuador. They could have taken an easier road. On October 28, 1949, Elliot wrote in his journal, "He is no fool who gives what he cannot keep to gain that which he cannot lose." He knew the highest level of faith. Do you? Will you still serve Him if it cost you something?

Graphically warned by a prophet that he would be imprisoned if he went to Jerusalem, Paul replied, "for I am ready not to be bound only, but also to die at Jerusalem for the name of the Lord Jesus" (Acts 21:13). Obedience was better than deliverance. It always is.

To believe that God is real is fundamental to faith. To serve Him is even greater. Greater yet is to believe that He is able to deliver—even deliver you. But, the greatest faith of all is to be faithful, to serve Him when it costs you something, or even when it costs you everything.

Faithful New Testament believers living at the fifth level of faith could lose their lives for Christ. He lost His for them, could they expect any less?

They obey. They do His will, not their own.

They deny themselves.

They die to the flesh, its pleasures and lusts.

Daily, they take up a cross.

This army of Christ will never be satisfied with a costless and worthless faith.

Whey many around them drift toward religious insanity, they stand for truth. They will never lose their minds.

May this same mind be in you.

If God has spoken to you through this book and you believe it is a prophetic word for the modern Pentecostal church, please help us distribute it to as many people as possible. Write today for ordering information and quantity discounts.

Larry E. Martin
P.O. Box 36355
Pensacola, FL 32516

mail@drlarrymartin.org

ABOUT THE AUTHOR

In 2012, Dr. Larry Martin (Doc Martin) celebrated his forty-fifth year of gospel ministry. He has spent almost twenty-five years pastoring churches in Oklahoma, Texas, Florida, and Tennessee. While still in his teens, Martin launched his ministry career as a traveling evangelist. He went back to itinerate evangelism from 1997 until the end of 2004. For three years he returned to the pastorate and then answered the call to a new missionary/evangelistic venture in early 2008. He has travelled throughout the United States and in more than fifty nations.

Born and raised in the Assemblies of God, Martin is distinctively Pentecostal. He often refers to himself as a "hard-shell holy roller." Thousands have received the baptism in the Holy Ghost during his ministry.

Martin has attended eleven different institutions of higher education. He is a graduate of Cameron University, Oklahoma Missionary Baptist College, Southwestern Oklahoma State University, and The Assemblies of God Theological Seminary. His last degree earned was the Doctor of Ministry at Austin Presbyterian Theological Seminary in Austin, Texas.

In 1994, Martin was chosen as the president of Messenger College in Joplin, Missouri. Previously, he also served the college as the Dean of the School of Lifelong Learning and as a professor of theology and missions.

From 2001-2004, Martin served Brownsville Revival School of Ministry in Pensacola, Florida as Academic Dean. He taught a number of courses in the college and was a speaker at the Brownsville Assembly of God Church.

Also a free-lance writer, Martin's articles have appeared in *Charisma, The Remnant, Ministries Today, Pulpit Helps, The Missionary Voice, The International Pentecostal Holiness Advocate, The Pentecostal Messenger, The Pentecostal Minister, The Message of the Open Bible, The Pentecostal Leader, The Church Herald and Holiness Banner, The Brownsville Report, The Church of God Evangel* and others.

Martin, considered by many to be an authority on the Pentecostal revival at Azusa Street, is the author of *The Life and Ministry of William J. Seymour* and editor of The Complete Azusa Street Library. He has written *In the Beginning,* a history of early Pentecostalism; *We've Come this Far by Faith* on the founding of the Pentecostal Church of God; *For Sale the Soul of a Nation, The Topeka Outpouring of 1901*; and has edited and/or contributed to several other works.

Highlights of Martin's ministry include speaking at the Azusa Street Centennial in Los Angeles and the Welsh Revival Centennial at the University of Wales in Bangor. Martin also preached at the IPC Convention in Kumbanad, India, for years billed as the largest Pentecostal gathering in the world. In 2012, he led a crusade in Medakenya, Ethiopia where 40,000 people made a confession of faith in Christ. Martin is comfortable speaking to ten or ten thousand.

River of Revival Ministries, Inc. (RRMI) was founded by Martin and he continues to serve as president of the ministry. Christian Life Books, the publishing arm of RRMI has published more than forty titles on revival and related subjects.

Martin is married to Tajuana Jo (T. J.), who is his loving partner in both life and ministry. The couple have two children, Matthew Dallas who lives in Cape Girardeau, Missouri; Summer Jo, who lives in Pensacola; and, one grandson, Matthew Dallas Martin II, also in Cape Girardeau.

Dr. Larry Martin
2012 Medakenya, Ethiopia Crusade
River of Revival Ministries, Inc.

The Complete Azusa Street Library

The Life and Ministry of William J. Seymour
LARRY MARTIN

How Pentecost Came to Los Angeles
Frank Bartleman

THE APOSTOLIC FAITH

Pentecost Has Come

The Comforter Has Come!

WWW.AZUSASTREET.ORG

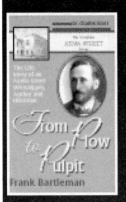

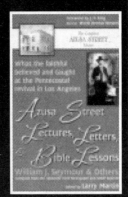

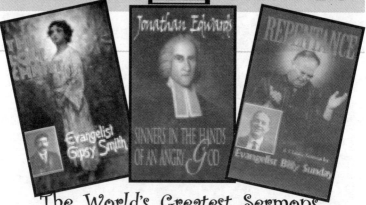

"... through faith, though he is dead, he still speaks." Hebrews 11:4

CARRIED BY ANGELS!

LEONARD RAVENHILL
1907 — 1994

"ARE THE THINGS YOU ARE LIVING FOR
WORTH CHRIST DYING FOR?"

Christian Life Books is honored to make available classic books by Leonard Ravenhill. Each book, in its own way, will convict you and draw you to a closer walk with God. No one in the Twentieth Century, prayed more, believed more, or worked more for revival in America and his native England than Leonard Ravenhill. Speaking from the grave, his words are as powerful today as when the ink fell from the pen of this anointed man of God.

Logging some 150,000+ miles a year and often speaking with over half-a-million young people annually, Winkie Pratney has wide experience in youth work. His technical background in both science and the popular music culture has given him a unique insight to the particular needs of a media-dominated technological society, and his constant monitoring of youth trends combined with continual feedback from young people themselves has helped him interpret these for those with a vital interest in the welfare of the young. Besides annual leadership training seminars he has for three decades helped challenge and inspire young people to holy and happy living.

A frequent featured speaker and guest on national television talk shows, his audio and video-tape lectures are carried by many effective outreach ministries as part of their training. Winkie has authored more than twelve books including youth manuals like the best-selling *Youth Aflame!*, *Handbook For Followers Of Jesus*, books on contemporary and historical issues like *Devil Take The Youngest*, *Dealing With Doubt* and evangelistic and apologetic works like the contemporary devotional theology *The Nature And Character Of God*.

❦

Histories of the world's greatest revivals!

Biographies of the revivalists!

Proven principles to change the world!

❦

When the question is asked: "What hinders revival?" one of the simple answers is this: We do not have men and women who are prepared to pay the same price to preach the same message and have the same power as those revivalists of the past. Without these firm believers, the community can never be changed. We say we want revival. But who today is prepared to live a life of absolute obedience to the Holy Spirit, tackling sin in the church as well as the streets, preaching such a message of perfection of heart and holiness of life—a message feared and hated by the religious and street sinner alike?